THE BAPTIST ALMANAC AND REPOSITORY OF INDISPENSABLE KNOWLEDGE

THE BAPTIST ALMANAC AND REPOSITORY OF INDISPENSABLE KNOWLEDGE

☙

Being a compendium of events both amazing and amusing of that great host known far and wide as Baptists

☙

Wherein is contained in anecdoctal form the record of the trials and triumphs, the ebb and flow, the great and the small, the tragic and the comic of Baptists from their beginnings in America until the dawn of the modern era

☙

With particular attention to that peculiar people of God known as Southern Baptists

REUBEN HERRING

BROADMAN PRESS
NASHVILLE, TENNESSEE

4265-21

ISBN: 0-8054-6521-9

Illustrations on these pages—24, 28, 31, 41, 45, 46, 48, 51, 59, 63, 96, 113, 117, 120—are by Erwin Hearne and are used by courtesy of the Historical Commission, Southern Baptist Convention, Lynn E. May, Jr., Director.

Layout and Design: O. Dixon Waters

Subject headings: BAPTISTS—HISTORY

Dewey Decimal Classification: 286.08

Library of Congress Catalog Card Number: 75-35397

Printed in the United States of America

To Our Five Sons

Widespread ignorance of our Baptist heritage is one of the most critical issues facing Southern Baptist churches in the 1980's.

The IMPACT '80's Emphasis Plan, adopted by the Convention at Miami Beach in 1975, noted that "widespread ignorance of Baptist . . . heritage affects the unity, the fellowship, the loyalty, and the polity of the churches." Only the family, church leadership, Bible study, and church planning were listed ahead of the concern for Baptist heritage as the most critical issues facing the churches in the '80's.

The plan noted that "Baptists have a unique and distinctive heritage" which not all Baptists understand or appreciate. From 1943 to 1974, membership of Southern Baptist churches doubled. Many of these new converts are ignorant of the distinct contribution Baptists have made to the life of America and to freedom-loving people everywhere.

To develop a greater appreciation for our heritage, a three-year "Baptist Way" emphasis is planned for Southern Baptist churches in the '80's.

It would indeed be tragic if the rich heritage of Baptists should ever be neglected or taken for granted. Students of government have noted that the most significant difference between governments in Europe and the United States is the principle of separation of church and state in the United States Constitution.

Baptists may claim a major share of the credit for this unique contribution to the government of nations. More than any other religious group, Baptists have fought for the principle of separation of church and state. They suffered persecution at the hands of the state-supported church from New England to Georgia until the nineteenth century.

When governmental support for all churches, rather than only one favored church, was offered, Baptists stood alone as a religious body in rejecting this proposal. Baptists correctly foresaw that the separation principle would be a better safeguard for religious freedom than state support.

This selection of vignettes from the Baptist story in America presents only some highlights and sidelights rather than the complete story. It is hoped that these brief glimpses of pivotal events, as well as behind-the-scenes incidents, will make a readable story that will whet the reader's appetite for more information about his glorious past.

The story is given a light touch, with the conviction that Baptists not only are aware that they are but sinners saved by grace, but also are big enough to laugh at themselves.

REUBEN HERRING
1976

Contents

11

The Lash of Persecution

HOW "Swearing John" Became a New Man

"Swearing John Waller," a man once known to his rowdy friends as opposed to all forms of religion, became a new man. Instead of opposing religion, he became a Baptist preacher in Virginia at a time when Baptist preachers were persecuted by the state.

Waller's life was changed after he served as a member of a grand jury hearing charges against Lewis Craig, a Baptist preacher. The grand jury indicted Craig for preaching the Baptist gospel and holding unlawful worship services without permission of the state-supported church of Virginia.

Following the hearing, the grand jury retired to a tavern. There Craig boldly faced his accusers.

"When I was in all kinds of folly and vice," Craig told the men, "the courts took no notice of me. But now that I have forsaken all those vices and am warning men to forsake and repent of their sins, you bring me to the bar as a common criminal. How do you explain all this?"

The grand jury could not answer the Baptist preacher's counter charges. And Waller could not get away from Craig's boldness. For eight months he pondered the difference between his life and that of Lewis Craig. He began to attend church and to listen to other Baptist preachers. At last he made a profession of faith, was baptized, and began preaching the Baptist gospel that he once persecuted.

TWENTY-EIGHT Baptists Arrested for Refusal to Pay Tax

Twenty-eight Baptists were arrested and imprisoned in Massachusetts prior to the Revolutionary War for refusal to pay a clergy tax for the support of ministers of the state church.

Massachusetts townships levied a tax on all inhabitants and estates within the township for the support of "orthodox ministers." Many Baptists were arrested and otherwise persecuted in Massachusetts for refusal to pay the tax.

Four tax assessors also were imprisoned for failure to include the clergy tax in their assessments. Even these public officials regarded the tax as unjust.

The tax "for the support and settlement" of ministers of the state-supported church was general throughout colonial Massachusetts, except in Boston. Bostonians were exempt through the influence of Cotton Mather, a powerful leader of the established church who saw in the tax a threat to his position.

CONNECTICUT Passed Laws to Keep Out Evangelists

In order to prevent the spread of the free church in the state, Connecticut passed laws—before the American Revolution—prohibiting traveling evangelists from preaching there and fining members of the state church for attending their services.

Because traveling evangelists were winning many converts away from the state church in Connecticut, the established church succeeded in having a law passed with the following penalties:

- *No evangelist was allowed to preach in the parish of an established church without permission. Penalty was imprisonment until payment of a one hundred pound bond, to be forfeited in the event of further violation.*
- *A nonresident evangelist who preached in Connecticut without permission was arrested and deported as a vagrant.*

- *No recognized minister in Connecticut could preach in the parish of another minister without the latter's consent.*
- *Any person who withdrew from an established church to attend worship outside his congregation was fined ten shillings.*

One Connecticut pastor who visited a Baptist church to preach was arrested for disorderly conduct. When he asked his accusers how he was disorderly in preaching to a congregation at the invitation of their pastor, he was told that the Baptists were not an orderly society but a "disorderly company."

The state-supported church in Connecticut particularly objected to the doctrine of individual regeneration and profession of faith as preached by the traveling evangelists.

LAWYER Preached Gospel in Defiance of Law

When Connecticut passed a law during pre-Revolutionary War days that hindered the free exercise of religion, a lawyer decided it was time to take the law into his own hands.

Elisha Paine, then one of the leading lawyers in Connecticut, took down his shingle, left the courts, and set out to preach the gospel himself in defiance of a law that he knew to be unjust. The law prohibited traveling evangelists from preaching without permission of the state church of Connecticut and fined members of the state church who listened to them.

The lawyer-turned-preacher soon ran afoul of the law. He was twice arrested as an itinerant preacher and charged with "mocking or mimicking" a minister of the gospel. When four Connecticut ministers certified that Paine was qualified to preach, the trumped-up charges were dropped.

While he was imprisoned, Paine paid his jailer for the freedom of the jail grounds. There he preached to such large crowds that authorities decided he was less a threat to the state church while free than while in jail.

Following his release, Paine embarked on a five-month tour of New England during which he preached 244 "illegal" sermons.

PREACHER Talked His Way to Freedom

Seldom has a minister spoken with more feeling–or with better results—than did a Baptist evangelist in Virginia in 1772 when he talked a mob out of taking him to jail.

John Koontz was often persecuted by the state church in Virginia. Koontz had just begun a worship service when a mob appeared. Mobs led by or spurred on by the state-supported church frequently disrupted Baptist meetings in Virginia. Many Baptist preachers were arrested for preaching without a license from the state church.

"Take heed what you do," Koontz warned his captors as they led him away. "If I am a man of God, then you fight against God!"

The preacher's words brought conviction. Those of the mob who had heard the Baptist preach had no doubt that he was a man of God. One by one the mob began to disperse until Koontz was free to go his way and preach again.

CHURCH Leaders Arrested For Worship in Connecticut

Several preachers and members of their independent church were imprisoned and their property confiscated in 1748 for daring to oppose the authority of the state-supported church in Connecticut.

The trouble arose following a split in the established church of Canterbury, Connecticut. Several members of the church withdrew and formed an independent church, calling Thomas Marsh as their pastor. Before Marsh could be ordained, he was seized and imprisoned "for preaching without permission of parish ministers." When Marsh was released six months later, the independent church went ahead with his ordination and free worship.

Incensed by this defiance, a convocation of the established church ordered leaders of the independent church to appear before them to answer charges. When the independents refused to appear, four were arrested and jailed for periods ranging from a fortnight to eleven months.

WIDOW Taken to Jail for Resisting Church

A fifty-four-year-old widow spent thirteen days in jail in 1752 for refusal to pay a clergy tax for the support of a minister of the state church of Connecticut.

"It was about nine o'clock at night," Elizabeth Backus recalled, "when there was a knock at my door. I was expecting trouble because my son had already spent twenty days in jail for resisting the state church. When I refused to contribute to the salary of a minister who was not my pastor, I was taken off to jail."

Several years before, Mrs. Backus and others had withdrawn from the state-supported church when the minister began to receive members without evidence of regeneration and taught other doctrines which some members found objectionable.

Although she showed the effects of her ordeal, Mrs. Backus harbored no bitterness toward her persecutors.

"I could give up my name, estate, family, life, and breath to God," she said. "The prison looked like a palace to me. I bless God for all the laughs and scoffs made at me by my tormentors."

PATRICK HENRY Attacked Crown, Established Clergy

Amid cries of "Treason! Treason!" from a packed courtroom, a young lawyer named Patrick Henry denounced the meddling of King George III and pointed an accusing finger at the state-supported clergy of the established church.

Ordinarily the clergy of the established church received its salary in tobacco from the state of Virginia. When the price

Patrick Henry defends religious freedom.

of tobacco soared due to a crop failure, the Virginia legislature voted to give the ministers their salary in currency at a rate below the market value of tobacco.

Ministers of the state church appealed to King George III, who disallowed the act. When a state-supported minister sued for more salary, Patrick Henry fought the action in the Hanover County Court in 1763.

Henry told the court that when the king took action in behalf of the established clergy he "degenerated into a tyrant and forfeited all rights to his subjects' obedience." It was this charge that brought cries of treason from the courtroom.

Henry's powerful arguments won a moral victory. The jury awarded the plaintiff a token judgment of only one penny. The verdict was enthusiastically received by the people, who shared Henry's dislike for King George's high-handed legislation and had no respect for a "hired clergy" that took its problems to the crown.

The hearing was well attended by the established clergy, who had come to gloat over a victory. But as Henry attacked both crown and clergy, while courtroom and jury gave ill-concealed support, many clergymen left in haste before the decision was announced.

FLAG Raised Beyond Jail Wall Made Unusual "Call to Worship"

No congregation ever had a more unusual "call to worship" than that used by a group of Virginia Baptists in 1773.

The preacher, John Weatherford, was in Chesterfield County jail. He had been placed there, as many Baptist preachers of that day were jailed, for preaching without a license from the state church of Virginia.

Despite prison bars, Weatherford continued to preach to large crowds that gathered outside his cell window. Weatherford preached so effectively that authorities erected a crude stone wall some ten or twelve feet high—not to keep prisoners inside the jail, but to keep free men away from Weatherford's window. Jagged bits of glass were stuck on top of the wall to prevent Weatherford's hearers from climbing over.

The "call to worship" was a piece of cloth tied to a stick. When the Baptist preacher in his cell saw that flag raised above the wall, he knew that a crowd had gathered on the outside. It was his signal to begin preaching.

Nine converts of Weatherford's prison cell preaching were baptized at one time under cover of darkness, for fear the state-supported church might attempt to disrupt the service. Of course, the imprisoned Weatherford was unable to perform the baptism himself. For this service he called on another Baptist who had also braved persecution by the state church.

Weatherford was freed at last when Patrick Henry, that invaluable friend of oppressed Baptists, came to his defense. Weatherford attempted to pay Henry for his services by sending him five pounds in gold, carefully wrapped in a kerchief. But Henry returned the gold, still wrapped in the kerchief.

COLONEL Turned Preacher Found Military Experience Invaluable

A Baptist preacher who was a former colonel in the

Virginia militia found his military experience invaluable as he fought for religious freedom in Virginia shortly before the outbreak of the war for independence.

The minister, Samuel Harriss, encountered most of his opposition in Culpeper County, Virginia. The state-supported church of Virginia angrily persecuted any opposition in that area.

Harriss was the victim of mob violence on more than one occasion in Culpeper. Once as Harriss attempted to preach, he was told by the leader of a gang that he could not hold a meeting. When the congregation objected to this interruption, a fight broke out.

Fearing that Harriss might be injured in the melee, his friends spirited him away to a house and posted a guard at the door. Supporters of the state church followed, however, battered down the door, and would have beaten the Baptist preacher if he had not been rescued.

On another occasion when Harriss was conducting a meeting, a mob appeared carrying sticks, whips, and clubs. To avoid a brawl with state church followers, Harriss moved his meeting to another place.

Harriss was opposed by both the lawless and the law for preaching the Baptist gospel in Virginia. He was arrested for disturbing the peace and was charged with being "a vagabond, a heretic, a schismatic, and a mover of sedition everywhere." "Disturbing the peace" was the usual charge made against Baptist preachers in Virginia for preaching without a license from the state church.

PRISON Bars Could Not Silence Baptists Who Preached Gospel

Five Baptists who were arrested for preaching the gospel were released several weeks later when authorities found that prison bars could not silence their witness.

Long ignored as bothersome but insignificant, Baptists were persecuted in Virginia when they came to be regarded as a threat to the state church. While there was no law in colonial Virginia against preaching the Baptist gospel, ministers were required to be licensed by the state-supported church.

The five Baptists, four preachers and a layman, were arrested and charged with being "great disturbers of the peace." The prosecuting attorney accused the five of the crime of not approaching a man on the road without trying to "ram a text of Scripture down his throat."

The accused were promised freedom if they would pledge not to preach again for a year and a day. When they promptly refused, they were ordered jailed indefinitely.

Authorities were forewarned of events to come when the prisoners sang hymns as they were led to jail. The willingness of the Baptists to suffer for their convictions made a deep impression on bystanders.

When one of the five was released four weeks later, he appealed to the governor of Virginia in behalf of his fellow prisoners. He was granted an audience with the deputy governor and won him completely to the Baptist cause.

"You may not molest these conscientious people so long as they behave themselves in a manner becoming pious Christians and in obedience to the law," the deputy governor wrote the prosecuting attorney. Besides, he added, "persecuting dissenters only increases their numbers."

The deputy governor was a prophet. Before the Baptists were released, they preached to crowds outside the prison. While some tried to shout them down, others listened and were converted.

BAPTIST Property Seized to Build State Church

Almost four hundred acres of land belonging to Baptists, and valued at more than three hundred pounds, was confiscated in Massachusetts (1770) in order to build a meetinghouse for the state church. Even a Baptist cemetery was included in the property seized.

"They have also sold a dwelling place and an orchard, pulled up our apple trees, thrown down our fences, and made our fields waste places," the Baptists charged as they petitioned the Massachusetts General Court for release from oppression by the state-supported church.

Several years after a Baptist church was organized in Huntstown, Massachusetts, the state church settled a minister there and planned erection of a meetinghouse. Baptists, including their minister, were taxed for support of the state church.

When Baptists claimed exemption from the tax as the first organized church in the community, the established order simply had the town incorporated under a new name.

If "perpetual exemption to all Baptists and their congregations" from such persecution was not granted immediately, the Baptists threatened "to send to the British courts for help if it cannot be had in America."

JAILED for Preaching, Baptist Survived Two Attempts on Life

Of all the cases of religious persecution in colonial Virginia, none was more violent than that involving James Ireland, a Baptist preacher.

While Ireland, a fearless crusader against the state church of Virginia, was held for five months in jail, two attempts were made on his life. Once his cell was blown up with gun powder. On another occasion the jailer attempted to poison the Baptist. Both times Ireland escaped unharmed.

While Ireland was in Culpeper County jail, crowds gathered outside his cell window to hear the Baptist gospel. Once, authorities rode horses into the crowd, trampling, beating, and threatening Ireland's listeners.

Ireland was arrested by sheriff's deputies while preaching

from a tabletop in an outdoor service. The meeting was being held at the home of a Baptist layman, who warned Ireland that authorities might try to break up the meeting. To protect the layman, Ireland asked to be shown his property line. There Ireland set up a table straddling the property line and preached from the tabletop, so that he was no more on the layman's property than anyone else's.

"Before the service," Ireland said later, "I sat down and counted the cost of liberty or prison. Having ventured all on Christ, I determined to suffer all for him."

Ireland was accused of preaching without authority from the state church of Virginia. He was released after a lawyer pointed out that he was charged with violating laws that had been repealed seventy years before.

In spite of torture, abuse, and insults during his unlawful imprisonment, Ireland's spirit was unbroken. In addition to preaching from his cell window, he wrote letters of encouragement to friends addressed "From My Palace in Culpeper."

WEALTHY Preacher Risked His Fortune for Gospel

Even two hundred years ago, money "talked," and at least one Baptist preacher enjoyed some of the benefits money offered.

Eleazer Clay, a Baptist preacher in Virginia, accumulated a fortune before entering the ministry. He was believed to be worth $100,000—quite a sum in that day—and was one of the wealthiest ministers in the colonies. His gifts helped to build the church where he was pastor.

Clay's stand showed unusual courage. Baptists of that day were bitterly persecuted in Virginia. For preaching the Baptist gospel, Clay risked his wealth, influence, and position.

Probably because of his wealth and prestige, Clay escaped persecution by either the state church or civil authorities. Many

Baptist preachers in Virginia were less fortunate.

Clay was threatened on one occasion when a man rode up to the house where he was preaching and announced that he had come to horsewhip the minister. Immediately a friend of Clay's rushed into the house to warn him of danger.

"I am the son of Charles Clay and fear no man," the preacher declared. "If I have to go out after the man, I will give him one of the worst whippings he ever had in his life."

When he saw that Clay could not be intimidated, the caller left. Clay was not afraid of a fight. As a boy of fourteen, he had joined British troops in fighting the French and Indians.

FOUR Put on Bread and Water For Refusal to Quit Preaching

After forty-six days in jail, during which they were at times on bread and water, four Baptist preachers of colonial Virginia were at last released because they could not be silenced. The Baptists were arrested for preaching without a license from the state church of Virginia.

When their followers heard that the imprisoned preachers had been placed on bread and water, they promptly responded to the need. The dank and flea-infested cells of the prisoners were soon so full of provisions that the preachers gave the surplus to the needy of the community.

The preachers were at first held in close confinement but later were given the freedom of the prison grounds. There they preached to large crowds. Spurred by the state-supported church, mobs attempted to break up the meetings by scattering the crowds and banging loudly on a drum.

The preachers were arrested in a raid on a Baptist meeting led by two sheriffs and a parson of the state church. Two Baptist laymen also were arrested in the raid but were released after one was beaten and warned to leave the county.

At their trial the preachers were told that they would be

released if they posted bond of seventy-five pounds each and promised not to preach in the county. This the Baptists refused to do, on the grounds that they "ought to obey God rather than men." At the time of their arrest, the Baptists told magistrates that they had authority "from above" to preach the gospel. This was not good enough for the magistrates, who recognized only the license of the state church.

During their confinement, one of the preachers became critically ill. Thinking that he was dying, the others petitioned authorities to release him so that he might be attended by friends. The request was ignored.

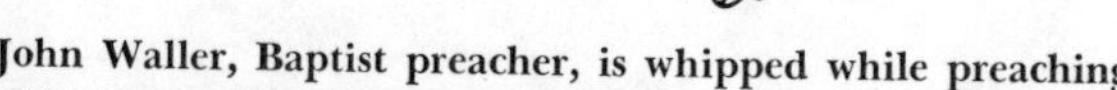

John Waller, Baptist preacher, is whipped while preaching.

HORSEWHIPPED by Sheriff, Preacher Returned to Pulpit

John Waller, a Baptist preacher in Virginia, had already spent more than a month in prison for preaching without permission of the state church. But even he could not have been prepared for the abuse he was to suffer on a spring morning in 1771.

As he opened an outdoor service, Waller was apprehensive when he saw three men approaching. It was the parson of the state church in the parish, the church clerk, and the sheriff.

As the congregation sang, the parson stepped on the platform with Waller and flipped the pages of the hymnal with his whip while the preacher tried to keep his finger on the selection.

Ignoring this disturbance, Waller next attempted to lead the opening prayer. As Waller prayed, the parson repeatedly stuck the butt of his whip in his mouth.

Seeing that the parson's attempts to halt the service were futile, the clerk of the state church stepped to the platform, seized Waller, dragged him from the pulpit, and delivered him to the sheriff who was standing nearby.

The sheriff no doubt was aware that the trio was guilty of unlawfully hindering a religious service. He added to their crime by unlimbering a horsewhip and in a rage gave the helpless preacher about twenty lashes. When the ordeal was over, Waller was covered with blood.

After the three intruders left, Waller found that he could still rise to his feet and returned to the pulpit. His hearers agreed afterward that he delivered one of the most powerful messages they had ever heard.

Before persecution, the Baptist cause scarcely flickered in Virginia. But fanned by messages of courage and faith, the flame of religious freedom soon burned brightly.

MOB Dipped Dogs to Ridicule Baptists

A mob attempted repeatedly to break up a Baptist meeting in Massachusetts during the time of the American Revolution.

The mob was no doubt inspired by the state church of Massachusetts. The state church persecuted Baptists for years and tried to stamp out freedom of worship in Massachusetts.

The Baptist congregation met in an open field near a river for worship and a baptismal service. During worship the mob arrived and attempted to break up the meeting. In ridiculing the Baptist stand on immersion, a dog was taken to the river and dipped while the mob roared approval.

The Baptists moved to another location and attempted to proceed with their services. The mob followed, however, and again mocked Baptist immersion by dipping dogs and one another.

A third time the Baptist congregation moved to escape the mob. Six candidates were baptized before the mob arrived and again broke up the meeting.

Law enforcement officers finally appeared, but instead of arresting mob leaders for hindering a worship service, they warned the Baptist preachers that they should leave town "for their own safety." Law enforcement officers and leaders of the state church often joined forces in persecuting Baptists in Massachusetts.

PRISON Bars Gave Way to Culpeper Church

For preaching the gospel, Nathaniel Saunders, a Baptist preacher, was imprisoned in Culpeper County jail (1773). Baptists were frequently imprisoned at that time for preaching without authority of the state church of Virginia.

At the time of his imprisonment, Saunders was pastor of the Mountponey Baptist Church. One hundred years later, the name of Saunders' church had been changed to Culpeper Baptist

Church. A church was erected on the site of the jail where Saunders had been imprisoned!

Saunders was not the only Baptist preacher to be imprisoned in Culpeper jail. Culpeper held more Baptist preachers who dared to preach in defiance of the state-supported church than any other jail in Virginia.

Among those who suffered for the cause of Christ in Culpeper were James Ireland, Elijah Craig, William McClannahan, John Corley, Thomas Ammon, Anthony Moffett, John Picket, Adam Banks, Thomas Maxfield, and John Dulany.

Although a church still stands on the site of the old Culpeper County jail, Culpeper Baptist Church had to move to larger quarters—proof that Nathaniel Saunders and his followers laid a firm foundation more than two hundred years ago.

BAPTISTS Threatened to Go to King in Fight To Secure Religious Freedom

Baptists in colonial Massachusetts had a ready answer when they were accused of disloyalty for threatening to take their grievances to King George. They pointed out that for the British Parliament to levy taxes on America was no more contrary to civil freedom than the Massachusetts clergy tax was contrary to religious freedom.

A persecuted minority, Baptists were fighting for survival in Massachusetts at the time. They opposed the state church, the tax levied for support of the state church clergy, and persecution of Baptists. They threatened to appeal to the British crown only as a last resort.

New Englanders were shocked when Baptists placed notices in local newspapers, calling on members of their group to present evidence of religious persecution. The announcement added that grievances would be presented to "another quarter than that to which repeated application has been made unsuccessfully and where complaints have been treated with indifference."

Baptists in Massachusetts protest persecution.

In protesting the state church in Massachusetts, Baptists set forth these principles:

- *The civil power does not have the right to set one religious group over another.*
- *The civil authority has assumed powers which rightly belong to the churches.*
- *By favoring one church and persecuting another, the government is interfering with freedom of choice in religious matters.*

LAYMAN Suffered Persecution For Religious Convictions

Thomas Waford, a layman in colonial Virginia, was not an ordained minister. But he had his own method of spreading the gospel.

A forerunner like John the Baptist, Waford went ahead of traveling preachers in Virginia to prepare the way for their coming. Waford first went into a community to arrange for a meeting. Then he publicized the news that a Baptist preacher was coming to hold worship services. By the time the preacher arrived, most of the community was prepared for his coming.

Like many Baptist preachers of his day, Waford suffered persecution because of his faith. The state-supported church in Virginia persecuted ministers who preached without a license from the state church. The state church also was responsible for the clergy tax for the support of ministers, and other abuses.

On one occasion after Waford had done his effective work as "advance man" for the coming Baptist evangelist, a mob arrived to break up the meeting. The mob was led by two deputies and a parson of the state church. Such gangs, either led by or spurred on by the state church, often broke up Baptist worship services in Virginia.

During the mob violence that followed, Waford was severely beaten and warned to leave the county immediately or face imprisonment.

CHURCH Was No "Sunday Night Place" for Baptists in Colonial Virginia

Baptist preachers of today who sometimes look in vain for their congregations on Sunday night must marvel at the zeal of Virginia Baptists of two centuries ago. They petitioned the Virginia House of Burgesses to protest a bill that would prohibit them from worshiping at night.

The bill to which Baptists objected also prohibited them

from fastening the doors of their meetinghouses, admitting slaves to their services, or baptizing slaves without permission of their masters.

Baptists also were prohibited by the bill from conducting worship services anywhere except at registered meetinghouses. These approved places of worship were limited to one per county.

James Madison, who frequently aided Baptists in their fight for religious freedom, observed "that liberal, catholic and equitable way of thinking, as to the rights of conscience, which is one of the characteristics of a free people . . . is but little known among the zealous adherents of our hierarchy. . . . Besides, the clergy are a numerous and powerful body, have great influence at home by reason of their connection with and dependence on the Bishops and Crown, and will naturally employ all their art and interest to depress their rising adversaries."

SOUTH CAROLINA Baptists Repaid Debt To New England Brethren

When Baptists in New England suffered persecution at the hands of the state-supported church and civil authorities two hundred years ago, their brethren in South Carolina had opportunity to repay a debt.

New England Baptists, particularly those in Massachusetts, were jailed, their property seized, and their lands and crops laid waste, and they were taxed for the support of the state church. When they appealed to other Baptists for financial aid, the Baptists of South Carolina were quick to respond.

The Carolinians had a close kinship with their northern brethren for almost one hundred years before American independence. A congregation from Maine established the first Baptist church in South Carolina.

Baptists made a brave attempt to establish a church in Kittery, Maine, in the late 1600's. They faced relentless persecution from the state-supported church and finally were driven

South Carolina Baptists aid New England brethren.

out. William Screven, pastor of the Kittery congregation, was arrested repeatedly for preaching the Baptist gospel, and members of his congregation were fined and otherwise persecuted for attending Baptist services. The pastor was threatened with banishment.

Screven and the First Baptist Church of Kittery finally left Maine as a body and settled in South Carolina in the 1680's. Although the New Englanders found life hard in the South Carolina wilderness, they discovered religious freedom worth any sacrifice. The church flourished, and in 1751, the Charleston Association was formed by four Baptist churches. The association pioneered in evangelism and education.

YOU Will Rot in Jail, Judge Threatened Minister

A Baptist preacher who was told by the presiding judge at his trial, "You shall lie in jail until you rot!" was released after being ably defended by Patrick Henry.

The minister, Jeremiah Moore, was arrested for preaching without authority from the state church of Virginia.

During his stirring defense of Moore, Henry cried, "Great God, gentlemen, a man in prison for preaching the gospel of the Son of God!"

Henry was not only a champion of liberty, but a defender of imprisoned and persecuted Baptists in colonial Virginia.

STATE Church Confiscated Baptist Deacon's Property

Three tons of hay and several bushels of rye were confiscated from the farm of an aged Baptist deacon in Massachusetts in 1799. The grain was sold and the money given for the support of a minister of the established church of the state.

The deacon, Abner Chase, had never been a member of the state-supported church.

For years Baptists of Massachusetts fought the oppression and unjust taxation of the established church. In 1795 six Baptists were arrested for refusal to pay the tax for the support of ministers of the state church. Considerable property of Baptists also was confiscated at that time.

When Baptists were instrumental in bringing about the adoption in 1789 of the First Amendment to the Constitution, they hoped that their long struggle for religious freedom in America was at an end. The amendment states that: "Congress shall make no law respecting an establishment of religion, or prohibiting the free exercise thereof." Ten years later that freedom was not yet secured in Massachusetts.

❧

WOMAN Aided Preacher In Flight from Catholics

Aided by a brave woman in his congregation, a Baptist preacher escaped exile to Mexico when Mississippi was under control of Spanish Catholics.

Because the Catholic hierarchy regarded the Baptists in Mississippi as a menace, they were ordered to "desist from their heretical psalm-singing, praying and preaching in public or they would be subjected to sundry pains and penalties." In 1795, the Spanish military commandant at Natchez issued the ultimatum that "if nine persons were found worshipping together except according to the forms of the Roman Catholic Church, they should suffer imprisonment."

The Baptist preacher, Richard Curtis, and other Baptists chose to ignore the warning. Curtis was arrested, and the commandant warned him that, unless he quit preaching, he and his followers would be exiled to Mexico.

After that, the Baptists worshiped only at night with a lookout on guard against intrusion. When a posse arrived to break up one of these meetings, Curtis realized that he must flee Mississippi or face exile. He and some of his followers decided to go to South Carolina.

Because any who aided Curtis and the others would also face exile, friends were reluctant to give the fugitives provisions for their flight. When no one volunteered help for Curtis, Chloe Holt came to his aid.

"If the men are so faint hearted that not one of them will take provisions to Dick Curtis and his companions in order that they might escape the clutches of the gospel-hating Catholics," she said, "then give me a good horse with a man's saddle and I will go in spite of the Spaniards, and they can catch me if they can."

Curtis and his friends remained in South Carolina for more than two years, but returned to Mississippi when the United

States acquired the territory from Spain and the Spanish Catholics lost their power.

☙

35

The Struggle for Religious Freedom

TEA PARTY Tax Not as Bad as Clergy Tax, Backus Wrote

The British tax on tea which led to the "Boston Tea Party" was not as bad as the clergy tax that Massachusetts imposed on Baptists, wrote Isaac Backus to the Massachusetts Assembly.

Isaac Backus

"All America is alarmed by the tea tax," wrote the Baptist leader in his forthright letter, "though, if they please, they can avoid it by not buying the tea; but we have no such liberty. We must either pay the little tax, or else your people appear, even in this time of extremity, determined to lay the great one upon us."

Backus referred to the clergy tax whereby Baptists must contribute to the support of ministers of the state church.

"These lines are written," he continued, "to let you know that Baptists will not pay the clergy tax, not only under your principle of taxation without representation, but because we dare not render homage to an earthly power which we are convinced belongs only to God.

"If you want to know what we ask of Massachusetts authorities," Backus concluded, "only allow us freely to enjoy the religious liberty that they do in Boston. We ask no more."

BAPTISTS Joined in Fighting First Skirmish of Revolution

The first skirmish in the fight for American independence may have been fought at Alamance Creek, North Carolina, on May 16, 1771. Baptists are believed to have joined in the fight, hoping to throw off oppression and win religious freedom.

Some two thousand colonists, perhaps less than half of them armed, engaged the state militia for about two hours. The poorly-armed woodsmen were dispersed, but they served notice that they were ready to fight and die for the cause of freedom.

The Regulators, as the rebels called themselves, banded together to oppose burdensome taxes and political corruption. Another issue between the Regulators and the royal government was a restriction prohibiting Baptist ministers in North Carolina from performing marriage ceremonies.

While Baptists were urged by their leaders not to take up arms against the government, it was believed that many joined the Regulators in fighting injustice. Throughout the colonies, Baptists responded to persecution by fighting boldly for religious and civil freedom.

Baptists began fighting for separation of church and state almost as soon as they arrived in America. Realizing that peaceful co-existence with the state church was not possible, Baptists joined in the fight for freedom. They hoped that in fighting with other colonists for civil rights, they might at the same time secure the religious freedom they were denied.

NEW ENGLAND Baptists Moved South with Gospel

Sixteen hardy New England pioneers, led by their pastor, Shubal Stearns, took the Baptist gospel to the South when they formed the Sandy Creek Baptist Church in the North Carolina wilderness in 1755.

Stearns and his congregation took with them the religion of regeneration and soul liberty so peculiarly suited to frontier people, but so bitterly persecuted by the established church in New England. Closely associated with Stearns in his work was his brother-in-law, Daniel Marshall.

Stearns was perhaps typical of the Baptist evangelists of his day. Small in stature and of limited education, he was a man of unusual natural gifts. He made effective use of piercing eyes and a voice that was melodious and powerful. As he preached, congregations were sometimes reduced to weeping and trembling.

Marshall was as zealous as Stearns. Although not an ordained minister, he served as a missionary to the Indians before going to North Carolina. Following his conversion, he had given away practically all of his possessions before he had begun preaching to the Indians.

Those who clung to the form and ritual of English and European churches were appalled that illiterate men such as Stearns and Marshall preached, that women prayed in public, and that Baptist services were sometimes a confusion of the wails of the convicted and the shouts of the converted. Yet this simple gospel, with its emphasis on the right of the individual to make his own peace with God, had a strong appeal to the freedom-loving people of the frontier.

BAPTISTS Won Right to Perform Marriages

While American troops were fighting the British in the war for American independence, the Baptists were scoring victories in their fight against the state-supported church.

A major victory for Baptists was won in Virginia with the passage of a law recognizing the validity of marriages performed by Baptist preachers. Prior to that time, marriages in Virginia were not legal unless they were performed "according to the rites and ceremonies of the Church of England," which was the Virginia state church.

Patrick Henry, long a friend of Baptists, had urged Baptist ministers to perform marriages without approval of the law. He believed that the best way to have the unjust law repealed was to ignore it. Some Baptists did not approve this strategy of "doing evil that good might come."

Baptists also led the fight for repeal of the tax to support ministers of the state church. The Virginia General Assembly ruled that "it is contrary to the principles of reason and justice that any should be compelled to contribute to the maintenance of a Church with which their conscience will not permit them to join, and from which they can therefore receive no benefit."

The General Assembly further decreed "that all dissenters of whatever denomination . . . shall . . . be totally free and exempt from all levies, taxes and impositions whatever towards supporting and maintaining said Church as it now is . . . established, and its ministers."

STRONG Opposition Faced Baptists in Fight For Religious Freedom

Baptists ran into stout opposition when they took their fight for religious freedom before the Continental Congress in Philadelphia in 1774.

John Adams said of the persecuted minority, "They might as well expect the stars to change their course as to expect Massachusetts to give up the established church."

Samuel Adams said that the Baptists making complaint were no more than "enthusiasts who make a show of suffering persecution."

Robert Paine also made light of the complaints, saying that exemption laws in Massachusetts had ended persecution and that no point of conscience was involved.

The Baptists stuck to their guns, however. Said one spokesman, "We claim and expect the liberty of worshiping God according to our conscience, not being obliged to support a ministry we cannot attend."

Baptists in many of the colonies fought the state-supported church and taxes levied for the support of the state church clergy. They stood firm in refusing to acknowledge that civil authorities had power which Baptists believe belongs only to God.

ALMOST to a Man, Baptists Joined in Fight for Freedom

Almost to a man, Baptists of two hundred years ago threw themselves into the fight for American independence.

Many Baptists enlisted with Gen. George Washington when he took charge of American troops. Even Baptist ministers joined the struggle for freedom, many serving as chaplains.

One reason for the all-out effort by Baptists was that they saw in the cause of civil liberty a hope for their own long-cherished dream: religious freedom. By joining the fight for independence, Baptists hoped to gain a favorable response to their cry for separation of church and state and soul liberty.

When Massachusetts authorities refused to grant Baptists release from the clergy tax which required them to contribute to support of the state church, Baptist leaders threatened to take their cause to King George. For this stand Baptists were accused of disloyalty and taking advantage of a critical situation to advance their own cause.

Isaac Backus, outstanding leader of Baptists in New England, answered this charge: "Baptist churches heartily unite with their countrymen in the cause of freedom and stand ready to exert all their abilities to defend it."

The Revolutionary War was a severe blow to many Baptist churches. With most of the men taking up arms and the entire population preoccupied with the fight for liberty, churches struggled for survival at a time when Baptists were beginning to gain strength and support in their fight for religious freedom.

HIS Messages Deadlier Than Musket, Baptist Preacher Told

A Baptist preacher who offered his services as a soldier in the Continental Army during the Revolutionary War was told to return to the pulpit because his messages were more effective against the enemy than a musket.

Richard Furman, who was to become the first president of the Triennial Convention, was ordained at nineteen and was twenty-one at the outbreak of the Revolution. He entered Charles-

Richard Furman flees British.

ton, South Carolina, in an army company led by his brother to volunteer for action against the British.

Furman would have become a soldier if authorities had not persuaded him that he was more valuable to the cause of freedom as a preacher than as a soldier. He was urged to return to the pulpit and continue to preach his powerful messages on soul liberty.

From stumps, barns, and pulpits, Furman preached. Many on the frontier were ignorant of current affairs and were still loyal to the crown. But as Furman pleaded the cause of liberty and religious freedom, they quickly reversed their loyalties and joined the fight for freedom.

When the British entered South Carolina, Furman was forced to flee to North Carolina and Virginia. Because of his influence, the British offered a reward for his capture.

BRAVE Chaplain Returned to Find His Church Had Become a Stable

Few soldiers in the Revolutionary War had a more outstanding record for bravery than John Gano, Baptist chaplain under Commander-in-Chief George Washington.

Although the chaplain's place was in the rear, Gano found himself in the thick of the fighting at the battle of Chatterton's Hill. The brigade in which he served was in panic, and some of the men were throwing down their arms and running.

"I somehow found myself at the front of the regiment," Gano explained afterward. "I dared not quit my post for fear of dampening the spirit of the soldiers or being accused of cowardice."

Gano was with Washington when the general announced the terms of the peace treaty to his troops. Washington called on the chaplain to lead in a prayer of thanksgiving. Washington and Gano were close friends, and many believe that Washington was baptized by the chaplain during the war.

John Gano

Gano was pastor of the First Baptist Church of New York City. He served as chaplain for the duration of the hostilities, and many men of his congregation enlisted with him when he joined the army.

When Gano returned to his church after eight years of military service, he found that his congregation of two hundred had been reduced to thirty-seven. He also found that the British had converted his meetinghouse into a stable.

BAPTISTS, State Church Were Foes During War for Independence

Baptists and the state-supported church, foes from the beginning in the colonies, again found themselves on opposite sides in the fight for American independence.

It was inevitable that the state church would side with the crown in the Revolutionary War. The British government had supported the state church and paid the salaries of the clergy by taxing the colonists, including Baptists.

Baptists, on the other hand, saw in the war for independence a fight for religious freedom as well. They were convinced that there could be no religious freedom as long as church and state were linked.

The state church fought bitterly to defend its favored position in the colonies. Ministers preached loyalty to the king from their pulpits and accused some in their congregations of treason.

One church was so incensed by these charges of treason that they seized their parson, dragged him from the pulpit, and whipped him outside the church.

Another clergyman of the state church took his pistols into the pulpit, announced that he would read all the prayers for the king and royal family, and warned that he would shoot anyone who tried to stop him.

Not all of the established clergy were so bold. Most closed their churches and fled before the war ended, many returning to England.

The clergy of the state church never gained the respect of the colonists. Some reached such a low moral state that the Virginia General Assembly provided for the sentencing of ministers who became "notoriously scandalous by drunkenness, swearing, fornication, or other heinous and crying sins."

BAPTIST Chaplains Active in War for Independence

Because of the large number of Baptists who enlisted in the fight for American independence, Baptist chaplains were permitted "to preach to the troops at convenient times without molestation or abuse."

Baptist chaplains were given freedom to preach after Virginia Baptists petitioned the Virginia Convention. The petition pointed out that Baptists and other dissenters did not wish to attend services conducted by chaplains of the state church.

In their petition Baptists explained that they had carefully considered what their part should be in the revolution and had agreed that "in some cases it is lawful to go to war." Military resistance against Great Britain was justified, the Virginia Baptists concluded, because of "unjust invasion, tyrannical oppression, and repeated hostilities against America" by the British.

The petition added that the question of enlistment in the armed forces was decided individually by Baptists.

PRAYERS of His Friends Called Preacher Back

Because the prayers of his friends called him back, one of the leading home missionaries of New England remained there to help form thirteen new Baptist churches.

Hezekiah Smith leaves on an evangelistic tour.

When Hezekiah Smith went to Massachusetts before the Revolutionary War, a church of another denomination asked him to fill their pulpit. When Smith revealed that he was a Baptist, there was dissension. Smith decided to leave for New Jersey.

Some of Smith's supporters tried to dissuade him from leaving Massachusetts. "If I return," said Smith, "your prayers will bring me back." As Smith was traveling by horseback to New Jersey, he stopped twice on his journey to meditate on the passage, "Strengthen ye the weak hands and confirm the feeble knees." At last he felt compelled to turn his horse back toward Massachusetts.

During the Revolution, Smith served for seven years as a brigade chaplain. He traveled throughout New England with the Baptist gospel, in addition to serving as pastor of one of the churches he organized. He often took members of his congregation with him on his evangelistic tours. For days and nights they traveled the backwoods trails of Massachusetts, Maine, and New Hampshire.

Smith also helped to organize the Warren Baptist Association, a powerful force for religious freedom in New England.

PRESIDENT WASHINGTON Told Baptists Religious Freedom Was Guaranteed

Baptists who declared that "liberty of conscience is dearer to us than property and life" appealed to newly-elected President George Washington to use his influence to secure religious liberty in America.

George Washington writes to assure Baptists of his stand for religious liberty.

Baptists were disturbed because they believed the new Constitution did not make "sufficient provision for the secure enjoyment of religious liberty." The General Committee of Virginia Baptists petitioned Washington to take action.

Long persecuted in Virginia by the state-supported church, Baptists told the President they were especially sensitive on the point of religious liberty "on account of the usage we received in Virginia under the British Government when mobs, bonds, fines, and prisons were our frequent repast."

Washington was quick to respond to the Baptist petition. "If I could now conceive that the General Government might ever be so administered as to render the liberty of conscience insecure," he replied, "I beg you will be persuaded no one would be more zealous than myself to establish effectual barriers against the horrors of spiritual tyranny and every species of religious persecution."

The President assured Virginia Baptists that he never would have signed the Constitution himself if he had entertained the slightest fear that it might endanger the religious rights of anyone.

"While I recollect with satisfaction that Baptists have been throughout America, uniformly and almost unanimously, the firm friends of civil liberty, and the persevering promoters of our glorious revolution," he added, "I cannot hesitate to believe that they will be faithful supporters of a free and yet efficient General Government."

Despite the assurance of President Washington, Baptists would continue their fight for religious freedom until the Bill of Rights was added to the Constitution.

BAPTIST Patriot Sacrificed Much in Fight for Freedom

In a denomination which, probably more than any other religious body, fought for American independence, few men suffered more than John Hart, a Baptist layman.

A champion of religious freedom and individual rights, Hart was elected to the Continental Congress, signed the Declaration of Independence, was elected vice-president of the New Jersey Congress, and was unanimously selected as speaker of the assembly under the new constitution of New Jersey.

Before the Revolutionary War, Hart owned a valuable farm and interest in a number of mills. His property was in the path of the armies of England and the colonies. During the fighting,

John Hart, Baptist layman, sacrificed all for religious freedom.

his crops were consumed, his stock driven away, and his farm and mills laid waste.

Hart's large family was scattered by the war, and the legislator was hunted as a traitor by British troops. For weeks he was a fugitive, hunted from house to house, spending the nights wherever he could find shelter, and often sleeping with farm animals.

The hardest blow of the war came when Hart's wife broke under the strain of the fighting. He was forced to flee from her bedside to escape capture, and she died during his absence.

Hart served in the New Jersey Assembly for ten years, where he militantly defended popular rights. He opposed the Stamp Act, favored an address to the king which declared that the right to tax belonged only to the colonies, and led opposition against providing for British troops in America.

He gave the land for the Baptist church in New Jersey where he and his family worshiped faithfully for many years.

SLAVE Church Accepted by Baptist Association

A church composed of Negro members and led by a Negro pastor was admitted to the Dover Baptist Association of Virginia in 1794.

The pastor was Gowan Pamphlet, once excluded from the association for preaching contrary to their rule prohibiting blacks from preaching. When Pamphlet was excluded from the association, he organized an independent church and continued to baptize and preach.

Slaves were admitted to membership in Baptist churches in Virginia. Some churches did not allow them a voice in business meetings, however.

Negro preachers were frequent victims of persecution for conducting meetings, and slaves were sometimes punished for attending these worship services. Mounted patrols sometimes interrupted services, chased down the slaves in attendance, whipped them, and then returned them to their masters.

Problems frequently arose in Baptist churches regarding slave members. A recurring question was what to do with slave owners who separated married slaves, and whether married slaves who were separated against their will should be allowed to remarry.

Another touchy question was whether slave owners should be disciplined when they were cruel to their slaves. It was generally agreed among Baptist churches that such offenders should be dealt with in the same manner as members guilty of other crimes.

❧

BAPTISTS Opposed Tax to Support All Churches

Having successfully led a fight to repeal taxation for the support of the state church, Virginia Baptists of 1785 fought a proposed *tax to support all churches.* The tax would affect all citizens, who would be allowed to designate the church or minister to whom the assessment would be paid.

Declaring the bill "repugnant to the spirit of the Gospel," the General Committee of Virginia Baptists called on Baptists throughout the state to petition the General Assembly against the bill.

"No human laws ought to be established for this purpose," the Baptists resolved, "but every person ought to be left entirely free in respect to matters of religion. The Gospel wants not the feeble arm of man for its support."

"Should the Legislature assume the right of taxing the people for the support of the Gospel," Baptists declared, "it will be destructive to religious liberty."

Baptists were aided in their fight by Thomas Jefferson, James Madison, and George Mason, leading Virginia statesmen of that day and courageous fighters for civil and religious freedom.

THOMAS JEFFERSON, Baptists United to Secure Religious Freedom

The statesmanship of Thomas Jefferson and the zeal of Virginia Baptists proved a winning combination. They teamed up to produce an "Act to Establish Religious Freedom," which at last assured liberty of conscience in Virginia in 1785.

Jefferson's beautifully worded declaration, adopted by the Virginia General Assembly, read in part: "No man shall be compelled to frequent or support any religious worship, place, or ministry whatsover, nor shall otherwise suffer on account of his religious opinion or belief; but that all men shall be free to profess and by argument to maintain their opinions in matters of religion, and that the same shall in no wise diminish, enlarge, or affect their civil capacities."

The Act to Establish Religious Freedom grew out of opposition, principally by Baptists, to a bill that would tax all citizens of Virginia for the support of the churches. Until that time only the established church had been supported by the state.

While Baptists had some support from other denominations

Baptists rejoice at the news of religious freedom in Virginia.

in other issues involving religious freedom, they stood alone in opposing the tax to support all churches. Other groups had become divided as the threat to religious freedom was overshadowed by the promise of state support for all religions.

At that time, only Baptists believed that separation of church and state was more vital to religious freedom than state support of churches. Fortunately, many other religious bodies came to see the wisdom of the Baptist position in the century that followed.

THOMAS JEFFERSON Was "Big Cheese" with Baptists

When Thomas Jefferson was inaugurated as president, Baptists showed him what a large place he held in their affections by presenting him with a mammoth cheese, no doubt the largest ever seen in the capital.

Made by the women of a Massachusetts Baptist church, the cheese weighed nine hundred pounds! It was presented to Jefferson by John Leland, a Baptist preacher and an old friend of the president.

Although Jefferson was not a Baptist, he early won the

admiration of Baptists. It was Jefferson who drew up an "Act to Establish Religious Freedom" in Virginia, thus freeing Baptists from persecution by the established church in that state.

Baptists also are indebted to Jefferson and other statesmen for support as they stood alone as a religious body in their fight for the First Amendment to the Constitution, which insures the "free exercise" of worship.

Jefferson, in turn, was indebted to Baptists. When he lived in Virginia, he frequently visited a small Baptist church. While observing the successful application of democratic principles by that body, Jefferson began to form beliefs which he later spelled out in the Declaration of Independence.

GIVE Us More Freedom, Baptists Told Constitution Framers

While many colonists were excited about the proposed new Constitution and the prospect of freedom from England, Baptists generally found the Constitution lacking.

Although the Constitution proposed to "secure the blessings of liberty to ourselves and our posterity," Baptists believed that the new document did not offer enough liberty.

The General Committee of Virginia Baptists agreed unanimously that the proposed Constitution did not make "sufficient provision for the secure enjoyment of religious liberty."

Religious liberty was the primary concern of colonial Baptists. They had suffered religious persecution throughout the colonies for a hundred years. In criticizing the Constitution, Baptists pointed out that it made no provision whatsoever for religious liberty and contained only one incidental reference to religion.

Patrick Henry, an old friend of Baptists, supported them in their stand against the new Constitution and added that he thought the document "squinted at monarchy."

Baptists were to continue their fight until they secured adoption of the Bill of Rights with its First Amendment declaring that "Congress shall make no law respecting an establishment of religion, or prohibiting the free exercise thereof."

Roger Williams and Indians.

BAPTIST Dream of Religious Freedom Realized at Last in Bill of Rights

That part of the United States Constitution known as the "Bill of Rights" and which begins, "Congress shall make no law respecting an establishment of religion, or prohibiting the free exercise thereof," was a major victory for Baptists.

It was a victory for Roger Williams, banished from Massachusetts into a frozen wilderness because of his "dangerous" religious convictions, 150 years before the Bill of Rights was passed.

It was a victory for Obadiah Holmes, given thirty lashes in a public whipping in Boston for conducting illegal Baptist worship services a century before the republic was born.

It was a victory for scores of Baptists from Georgia to New England, who suffered fines, imprisonment, beatings, insults, loss of property, and bodily harm because of their religious convictions.

More directly, the First Amendment to the Constitution represented a victory for Virginia Baptists. They had petitioned President Washington, shortly before the Bill of Rights was presented to the First Congress, asking him to correct what they regarded as a fundamental weakness in the Constitution.

For Baptists, the civil liberties guaranteed in the Constitution meant little without the religious liberty guaranteed by the First Amendment.

PREACHER Played Key Role In Adoption of Constitution

A simple Baptist preacher played a key role in the adoption of the new United States Constitution in 1789.

John Leland

The preacher, John Leland, never held public office. Neither was he a delegate to a constitutional convention. Yet, he was one of the most popular preachers in Virginia and a Baptist spokesman for religious liberty.

When the Constitution was first submitted to the states for ratification, two leading Virginia statesmen—both staunch friends of Baptists—were on opposing sides. Patrick Henry opposed the Constitution, charging that it "squinted toward monarchy" and failed to insure individual rights. James Madison supported it, fearing that if it were not adopted, hopes for a unified republic would be lost.

County delegates were to be sent to a Virginia convention that would either adopt or reject the Constitution. Both Leland and Madison were candidates from Orange County, Virginia. Friends of Leland had persuaded him to run—opposing the Constitution on grounds that it failed to assure religious liberty.

While Madison was in Philadelphia on business, Leland's campaign gained momentum. By the time the statesman returned home, Leland's election as a convention delegate seemed assured. Madison went to Leland and presented his case for adoption of the Constitution. Leland withdrew from the race, and Madison was elected.

At the Virginia Constitutional Convention, Patrick Henry's flaming oratory would have consumed all hopes for ratification had it not been for Madison's powerful influence. Virginia favored the Constitution in a close vote.

Had Leland rather than Madison attended the convention, Virginia's decisive vote almost certainly would have gone against the Constitution.

MUSKET in Hand, Seventy-Year-Old Pastor Was Ready to Fight

In colonial America, Baptist preachers had to be fighters. And John Courtney, pastor of the Richmond, Virginia, Baptist Church for thirty-six years, was a fighter.

He fought for religious freedom against the Virginia state church. He served in the Continental Army during the Revolution. And during the War of 1812, the Baptist pastor, then over seventy, appeared in the public square, musket in hand, when it was thought Richmond was threatened.

Courtney did not receive a stipulated salary from his church but supported his family by working as a carpenter. A "hat collection" was taken at the close of each Lord's Day service, and the money was put in a handkerchief and taken by the chief deacon to the pastor's house where it was placed in a bowl.

The Courtneys lived in a house which the pastor rented for $25 a year, and the women of the church gave the family clothing. When a deed to the house and lot where the Courtneys lived was given to the pastor, he immediately disposed of the deed. Courtney did not want to run the risk of being identified with ministers of the established church of Virginia, whose handsome salaries were paid by taxes.

The Richmond pastor labored among all classes, including blacks, prisoners, soldiers, and others. He served as a home missionary on the Virginia frontier.

After he was too feeble to preach, Courtney continued to visit among his people. He would ride from house to house on his horse, call members of his flock to the door, and, still mounted, counsel with them and pray for them.

FOUR Great Statesmen Aided Baptists in Fight

Four leading American statesmen—George Washington, Thomas Jefferson, James Madison, and Patrick Henry—aided Baptists in their fight for religious freedom, finally realized in the First Amendment to the Constitution. Yet none of these men was a Baptist.

Washington was long a friend of Baptists. It was to him that Baptists appealed when they discovered that the Constitution lacked safeguards for religious freedom. Shortly after President Washington assured Baptists that "no one would be more zealous than myself" in the fight against religious persecution, the Bill of Rights was presented to Congress.

James Madison brought the Bill of Rights to Congress. He had advised Baptists to write Washington about the failure of the Constitution to secure religious liberty. He also drew up for Baptists a memorial to the Virginia General Assembly, protesting a general assessment for the support of religion.

Thomas Jefferson was a friend of John Leland, a leading Baptist spokesman for religious freedom. Although not a Baptist, Jefferson worshiped often in Baptist churches. He drew up an Act to Establish Religious Freedom, adopted by the Virginia General Assembly in 1785.

On more than one occasion, Patrick Henry, an eloquent lawyer, defended Baptists and the cause of religious freedom.

These four patriots fought with Baptists, not because they were themselves Baptists, but because there burned within them the same yearning for soul liberty that fired the Baptists of their day.

OVERTHROW of State Church Was Victory for Baptists

After suffering persecution at the hands of the state church in Virginia for decades, Baptists finally won a total victory in 1794. That year the Virginia General Assembly repealed all laws pertaining to religion except the "Act to Establish Religious Freedom."

This act, drawn up by Thomas Jefferson in 1785 at the urging of Baptists, stated that "all men shall be free to profess and by argument to maintain their opinions in matters of religion."

The action of the Virginia Assembly stripped the last traces of power from the state church. The last battle was fought over the right of the state clergy to glebes, homes and lands given to them by the government.

Baptists contended that the glebes should be sold and the money put to public use. They argued that the glebes not only belonged to the public because they had been purchased with tax money, but that the state had violated the principle of separation of church and state by giving property to the established church.

In overthrowing the established church in Virginia, Baptists won these advantages for themselves and others: freedom to worship without hindrance, exemption from taxes to support the state church, the right of ministers to preach without authority from the state church, authority of their ministers to perform marriages and other rites.

Baptists won these victories with little support from other dissenters. In their fight for sale of the glebes, for instance, Baptists appealed to Methodists and Presbyterians for support but were refused.

The established church fought to the finish for survival. From the pulpit, in the press, and wherever they found opportunity, the established clergy attacked Baptists. In one last, futile attempt to defend their favored position, clergy of the state church petitioned the Virginia General Assembly. They labeled Baptists as mad men with an "excess of religious enthusiasm without any knowledge of the Scriptures."

No One Fought Harder for Freedom than Backus

A Baptist preacher, Isaac Backus, probably did more than any other man to secure religious freedom in New England.

Backus wrote letters and petitions or appeared in person before the Continental Congress, state legislatures, Baptist groups, and wherever he could strike a blow for religious freedom or against religious oppression.

The Warren Baptist Association, which had as one of its aims the promotion of religious freedom in New England, employed Backus as a special agent. In ten years the evangelist traveled some 15,000 miles by horseback and preached almost 2,500 sermons in the interest of religious freedom.

Born into the established church in Connecticut, Backus

Isaac Backus takes the Baptist gospel to the Frontier.

withdrew because the church persecuted other religious bodies. He and those who withdrew with him formed an independent church which soon outnumbered the state church. The independents were taxed for the support of the state church, and in one year forty of the members, including some women, were imprisoned for opposing the established order.

Backus was baptized in 1751 and with six other baptized believers formed a Baptist church five years later. He concluded that "the Baptist way is certainly right, because nature fights so against it."

The Baptist patriot was as forceful with the pen as he was in the pulpit. He wrote almost constantly for liberty of conscience, separation of church and state, and against support of ministers by taxation.

61

The Call of the Frontier

TO Sing or Not to Sing Was Once a Familiar Tune

To sing or not to sing was a lively issue in many Baptist churches of the early nineteenth century. Even among Baptists who favored singing, many opposed the use of "machinery"—as musical instruments were sometimes called.

One of the musical instruments introduced into some Baptist churches as an aid to congregational singing was the bass viol. Some protested use of the "big fiddle" as unnecessary man-made machinery and a hindrance to worship.

Those who favored musical instruments took the time-honored Baptist position of citing the Bible as their authority. They pointed out that musical instruments had been used in worship since Old Testament times, quoting the Psalms and other passages for biblical support.

Those who opposed singing and the use of instruments also had tradition behind them. They pointed to the days of the early church and other times when Christians were persecuted. Forced to worship in secret, persecuted congregations could not sing for fear of being discovered. This custom of hushed and silent worship was still cherished by some.

Among "singing Baptists," congregational singing generally was led by the pastor or a church member with a strong voice. Due to the lack of hymnals, and because many in the congregations could not read, the leader usually read the lines of the hymn or psalm as the congregation sang.

This custom of "lining out" hymns was often performed

by a deacon, who stood in front of the pulpit. The term "deaconing" was sometimes used to describe the services of the song leader.

Revivals and camp meetings of that era did much to popularize singing and the use of musical instruments among Baptists, particularly in rural and frontier areas.

FIRST Baptist College Opened to All Denominations
Excluded from many colleges and universities of the state church, Baptists in America established their own institution of higher learning in 1764. The Baptist school, Rhode Island College, was opened to students "of all denominations or no denomination."

It is not surprising that Baptists established their first college in Rhode Island. Founded by Baptist Roger Williams, Rhode Island was one of the few colonies that allowed religious freedom. Williams settled in Rhode Island in 1636, after he was banished from the Massachusetts Bay colony for his views on religious freedom.

"Into this liberal institution shall never be admitted any religious tests," the Rhode Island College charter read. "On the

Rhode Island College is granted a charter.

contrary, all members shall enjoy free, absolute and uninterrupted liberty of conscience. Youths of all religious denominations shall be admitted to equal advantages and honors."

While the charter stipulated that the president and a majority of the trustees were to be Baptists, other officials and faculty members were to be selected "indifferently of any or all denominations."

The idea of the Baptist college originated within the Philadelphia Baptist Association. James Manning was the first president.

TO Evangelize Indians, Georgia Baptists Organized

To evangelize the Indians, encourage itinerant preaching, and organize Christian work throughout the state, the General Committee of Georgia Baptists was formed in 1803. This organization was the forerunner of the earliest state Baptist conventions in the South.

Jesse Mercer

The General Committee planned to send missionaries to the Creek Indians and to establish schools among the Indians as a first step in planting missions.

Itinerant preaching was largely responsible for the spread of Baptist work in Georgia around the turn of the nineteenth century. Preachers rode the backwoods trails, usually in pairs, building up weak churches and organizing new ones.

One of the hardest working of these itinerant preachers was

Jesse Mercer. In addition to his itinerant preaching and work among the Indians, Mercer was pastor of four churches. These churches baptized 149 converts in 1802.

Jesse was the son of Silas Mercer, another famous Baptist leader. When he was eighteen, Jesse was baptized by his father. He began preaching almost immediately and first conducted prayer meetings in the log cabin of his grandmother.

Although his own formal schooling was limited, Jesse Mercer gained stature among Baptists as a scholar and theologian. He was the founder of Mercer University.

TRAVELING Evangelist Believed Horse Only Slowed Him Down

A Baptist evangelist who may have been the first evangelical missionary to preach the gospel west of the Mississippi River did his traveling afoot.

The walking evangelist was John Clark. He did not bother to saddle a horse as he took the Baptist message to settlers of the western border. He believed that a horse only slowed him down.

Clark was one of the earliest evangelists in the west. He traveled hundreds of miles—afoot—to preach to frontiersmen in Missouri, Kentucky, and Illinois around the turn of the nineteenth century.

The rugged minister, whose calling demanded that he be as much scout and woodsman as preacher, was untiring in his efforts. He traveled for days along Indian trails and streams, not even stopping to rest at night if he had an urgent appointment at a distant settlement.

Once, well-meaning friends gave Clark a horse, saddle, and other equipment. But the minister was more concerned about the welfare of the animal than he was for himself. After a journey during which Clark spent much of his time seeing that the animal was well fed and rested, and was led safely across swollen streams and through other dangers, he pleaded with the owners to take their horse back. Clark was convinced that travel through the wilderness afoot not only was easier but faster.

SHERIFF Who Arrested Preacher Returned to Him for Baptism

A sheriff who once arrested a Baptist preacher came to him six years later for baptism.

The preacher was Daniel Marshall, a leading Baptist evangelist in the southern states at the time of the American Revolution. As Marshall was on his knees praying in an open-air meeting near Augusta, Georgia, he was arrested by Samuel Cartledge.

Marshall was arrested for preaching "contrary to the rites and ceremonies" of the state church. The state church persecuted Baptists from Georgia to New England until the First Amendment to the Constitution secured freedom of worship for all.

The sheriff never got away from his encounter with the Baptist preacher. As he was arrested, Marshall warned Cartledge to "be saved from your sins." Six years later the man who had persecuted Baptists was baptized into their fellowship.

SPIRIT of William Carey Present As American Baptists Organized for Missions

The spirit of William Carey, father of the foreign mission program of English Baptists, was present when Baptists in America organized for the support of foreign missions.

Carey was "represented" in America by William Staughton. Staughton was present in Kettering, England, when English Baptists formed the "Particular Baptist Society for the Propagation of the Gospel Amongst the Heathen" (1792). After Carey had urged, "Expect great things from God; attempt great things for God," English Baptists formed their society with a snuffbox treasury of fourteen pounds, two shillings, and six pence. Later Carey served as the society's first missionary to India.

Staughton never got away from the challenge of those days. When he sailed for America a few years later, he brought with him the missionary zeal of Carey.

When Luther Rice returned from the mission field to ask for Baptist support of the Judsons in Burma, Staughton rushed to his aid. He was instrumental with Rice in the formation of the General Missionary Convention in 1814 and was elected first corresponding secretary of the Baptist Board of Foreign Missions for the United States.

TRAVELING Baptist Church Found a Home in Wilderness

A Virginia congregation fearlessly pushed westward 600 miles through the wilderness from 1781 to 1783, forming Baptist churches along the way. The little band finally settled near Lexington, Kentucky, forming the first church in the wilderness north of the Kentucky River.

The church was led by Lewis Craig, a Baptist preacher who first gained attention for his fight for religious freedom in Virginia. Although he was imprisoned repeatedly in Virginia for preaching the Baptist gospel, Craig refused to be silenced.

When the Baptist leader saw that his fight for freedom was finished in Virginia, he took the gospel to the frontier. He formed seven new churches, three in Virginia and four in Kentucky.

When Craig left Virginia, he took most of his congregation with him. During the two years of their wilderness wanderings, the little group battled cold and rain, the dense and trackless frontier, and the constant threat of Indian attack. Craig took with him into the wilderness the same old Bible he had preached from in Virginia.

PREACHER Taken Captive In Raid on Settlement

A band of marauding Indians swept down on the little settlement of Severn's Valley, Kentucky, in 1782 and took captive a Baptist preacher before they could be driven off. It was believed that the captive was killed by the Indians.

The preacher, John Gerrard, had formed the Severn's Valley Baptist Church the year before, the first church organized on the Kentucky frontier. Gerrard had gathered the church in the shade of a large tree near the rude stockade the first settlers had built.

The congregation often worshiped in the open when weather permitted, always alert to danger. When they met indoors, a sentry was posted at the door and men worshiped with rifles and axes nearby.

Severn's Valley was one of the most formidable areas on the American frontier. Hostile Indians made it a bloody ground for settlers, and there was constant danger from attack. The fearless pioneers and their families had little time for farming, being engaged in clearing land, building defenses, and guarding against Indian attacks. Much of their food was taken from the wilderness.

UNBELIEVABLE $2000 Salary Received by Savannah Pastor

Baptist circles were buzzing as word spread quickly that a church in Savannah, Georgia, had called a pastor at the unbelievable salary of $2,000 a year. It probably was a record high salary for a Baptist preacher at the time, at the turn of the nineteenth century.

The preacher, Henry Holcombe, had been a captain in the cavalry during the Revolutionary War. He was called to preach while still in the service and preached his first sermon from horseback to his own troops.

Holcombe was a successful pastor in South Carolina before

going to Georgia. He was a member of the South Carolina Constitutional Convention that ratified the Constitution by a 2–1 majority.

To many Baptist preachers, particularly those on the frontier, Holcombe's salary was unbelievable. Many of them received no payment at all from their congregations. Others received only provisions or clothing.

An early meetinghouse.

PORTHOLES Instead of Stained Glass In Meetinghouses on the Frontier

Portholes took the place of stained glass windows in some Bapitst meetinghouses on the wilderness frontier. The portholes, similar to those cut in stockades on the frontier, enabled settlers to fire rifles at attacking Indians.

While part of the congregation worshiped, others stood watch at the portholes, ready to warn of attack and to open fire on the Indians. It was customary for Baptist congregations on the frontier to worship with weapons handy and to post lookouts at doors and windows of meetinghouses.

Squire and Samuel Boone, brothers of Daniel Boone, were members of a Baptist church on the Kentucky frontier. The church was organized by Captain William Bush, a friend of Boone's who sometimes accompanied him on his explorations.

When news reached the frontier of the surrender of Cornwallis, leader of British forces in America during the Revolution, settlements rang with celebration. This would lessen the threat of the Indians, who had allied with the British during the fighting.

SLAVE Whipped for Preaching

A former slave, who was whipped not long after the Revolution for preaching, was ordained in 1788 as pastor of the First Negro Baptist Church of Georgia. Located at Savannah, the church once was hindered and persecuted for worshiping.

The church was gathered by Abraham Marshall, Georgia's famous traveling preacher. In constituting the church, Marshall baptized forty-five converts in one day—probably a record even for Marshall.

The former slave, Andrew Bryan, said at the time he was whipped for preaching the gospel: "I rejoice not only to be whipped, but would freely suffer death for the cause of Christ."

Marshall also had his difficulties during the Revolution. He once was forced to flee from Georgia to North Carolina to escape the Tories. But he did not stop preaching the gospel along his escape route, even though his life was in danger.

ARMED Guard Protected Preacher from Indians

A congregation which was willing to risk its scalps to the Indians secured the services of one of the most famous preachers on the Kentucky frontier.

A Baptist church was formed at Owen's Fort, Kentucky, in 1785, but services were discontinued when Indian raids became frequent. When the congregation heard that the pastor of the Forks of the Elkhorn Baptist Church, William Hickman, might preach for them, they decided to try again.

An armed guard was sent to the Forks of the Elkhorn settlement to escort Hickman to Owen's Fort. The guard protected Hickman from Indian attack while he preached at several points and then gave him a safe escort home.

Hickman probably baptized more converts than any other Baptist evangelist on the Kentucky frontier. He preached a plain and solemn message, delivered in a voice like thunder.

In appreciation for his services, the church at Owen's Fort presented Hickman with several loads of grain—a handsome salary for a backwoods preacher.

PREACHER Who Used Notes Like Marksman Who Used Rest

"The preacher who can't stand up to a pulpit and preach without notes is no better than a marksman who can't shoot a rifle without a rest to steady his aim." This evaluation was voiced frequently among Baptist congregations around 1800.

The preacher who was no more "apt to teach" than to have to write out his sermons and read them must have missed his calling, many Baptists of that day believed. Although preachers of other denominations frequently used notes, Baptist congregations generally frowned on the practice.

Baptist preachers who did use notes sometimes attempted to hide them from their congregations. This bit of subterfuge often led to embarrassment. If the preacher's notes became covered up or fell to the floor, he sometimes had difficulty bringing his sermon to a satisfactory conclusion.

Baptists soon learned that this emphasis on extemporaneous speaking had its drawbacks. Preachers who entered the pulpit with no outline or notes found themselves preaching the same sermon over and over. The contents of this rambling message often ranged from Genesis to Revelation, touching on most of the prophets and epistles in between.

This practice soon opened the way for notes in the pulpit. There was one thing Baptist congregations liked even less than a preacher who used notes: a preacher who didn't know when he had finished!

FRONTIER Revival Doubled Some Churches Overnight

A revival that swept the frontier around 1800 and afterward doubled the membership of some Baptist churches almost overnight.

The revival centered in Kentucky, but was general throughout most sections of the country and touched most evangelical denominations. Methodists, Presbyterians, and Baptists probably were most affected.

The Great Crossing Church of Kentucky, organized in 1785—not many years after Daniel Boone entered Kentucky—was one example of what the revival did in Baptist churches. The church added only six members from 1795 to 1800. Then revival fires broke out. The church added 175 members in 1800 and 186 more in 1801.

Twenty-nine churches in the Elkhorn Association of Kentucky reported only twenty-nine conversions in 1799. Two years later more than 3,000 members were added by baptism, and nine new churches were formed.

Revivals lasted from a few days to a few weeks. It was in the camp meetings that many of the excesses occurred, such as jerking, falling, howling, fainting, and other emotional outbursts. Baptists did not join in the camp meetings as enthusiastically as some of the other denominations.

Many Baptist churches also were wary of the traveling revival preacher. He went from church to church, especially on the frontier, often with good results. He was opposed by some local pastors, and many churches objected to his "wholesale" methods of evangelism.

❧

BEHIND Plow or Pulpit, Frontier Preacher at Home

He had to be at home behind the plow as well as the pulpit and able to handle bullets as well as the Bible. These were some of the demands made of the frontier preacher on horseback.

Traveling over a frozen, snow-covered wilderness trail to take the gospel to frontier settlers was no task for a tenderfoot. Keep your tinderbox, flint, and steel handy, warned these backwoods evangelists, and keep your feet to the fire once you have a blaze going. And if you can't travel at least twenty-four hours on the trail without food, better turn your mount back toward the settlements.

Fired by a religious zeal to carry the Baptist message to every log cabin in the wilderness, these trail-riding preachers moved from one isolated settlement to the next. To keep alive, they learned to combine the skills of the farmer, the trapper, the long hunter, the trail blazer, and the woodsman.

Because he received little or no compensation for his labors, the intinerant preacher had to be self-supporting. Without his knowledge of the woods, he might die of exposure during a winter night on the trail. Or, if he survived the night, he might find himself too numb and near frozen to mount his horse and continue his journey to the next wilderness cabin.

❧

WITH Missionaries They Did Not Send Out, Baptists Organized for Foreign Missions

In one of the most unusual events in the history of Christian missions, Baptists in America suddenly found themselves with three foreign missionaries whom they had not sent forth.

Adoniram Judson

The missionaries were Adoniram Judson, his wife Ann, and Luther Rice. The three had sailed for India as missionaries of the Congregational church.

On the long sea voyage to India, Rice began to investigate the doctrine of believer's baptism and to study his New Testament on the subject. He arrived in India to find that the Judsons, who had made the voyage in another vessel, also had been disturbed by the question of baptism and were engaged in a similar prayerful study.

Not long after their arrival in India, first the Judsons and then Luther Rice were baptized. As they felt compelled to resign as Congregational missionaries, the trio found themselves in a strange country without financial backing.

The powerful British East India company forced the missionaries to leave India. It was agreed that the Judsons would go to Burma while Rice returned to America to make proper settlement with the Congregationalists and to try to enlist the support of Baptists.

Rice proved as effective a missionary at home as the Judsons were in Burma. At Philadelphia in 1814, Baptists in America organized "The General Missionary Convention of the Baptist Denomination in the United States for Foreign Missions." The influential Richard Furman, pastor of the First Baptist Church of Charleston, South Carolina, was elected first president of the Convention.

CONGREGATION Waited Six Hours To Hear Evangelist on Horseback

Congregations that begin to fidget when the preacher goes a few minutes past the hour could learn patience from frontier Baptists. One such congregation on the Missouri frontier once waited six hours for the preacher to arrive!

The worship service was to have started at noon. When the preacher failed to arrive at the appointed hour, the congregation of about twenty settlers waited—and waited.

The preacher, John Mason Peck, had started out for the wilderness church about dawn. He expected to cover the twenty miles on horseback in good time. But he became lost en route and had to retrace his steps many times in order to find the trail.

About sundown Peck arrived in the clearing where the congregation was gathered. As some of the settlers would have to travel several miles to their cabins before dark, Peck immediately launched into his sermon.

John Mason Peck

Afterward one of the settlers invited Peck to his cabin for a meal and lodging for the night. When his hostess asked the traveling preacher if he had eaten dinner, Peck replied, "I propose first to eat breakfast. Then we will talk about dinner and supper."

At dawn the next day, Peck had saddled his horse and was on his way to the next settlement fifteen miles away, where a Baptist congregation had not heard a preacher in six months.

TRAVELING Preacher Wounded In Flight from Indians

A traveling Baptist preacher narrowly escaped with his life when he was attacked by Indians on the Illinois-Kentucky frontier. His traveling companion was less fortunate.

The minister, David McLain, and his companion were traveling on horseback when they came to a river and an abandoned ferry. They had just swum the river with their horses when they were attacked by the Indians. In the first hail of bullets, McLain's companion was shot from his saddle and killed. McLain's horse was shot from under him.

"I threw my saddlebags into the brush and ran for my life," McLain said afterward. "I was poorly fixed for a foot race, however, as I had just crossed the river and was hindered by my spurs and wet boots, leggings, and an overcoat."

The preacher soon outdistanced all the Indians except one brave. When this one fired and missed, the preacher threw off his coat, hoping this prize would satisfy the Indian and he would give up the chase. The Indian continued in pursuit, however, and the life-and-death race continued through the wilderness for

David McLain escapes Indians.

more than an hour. During this time the Indian fired eight times at McLain. One of the balls struck the preacher near the elbow.

The race led to a stream and the preacher dived in. Here the Indian gave up the chase with a war whoop, evidently deciding that the water was too cold for a swim. On the other side of the stream, McLain rolled on the ground to restore circulation after his icy swim. Then, wounded and exhausted, he made his way through the wilderness to the nearest settlement —thirty-five miles away.

Some time after this incident, the Baptist preacher was approached by John Mason Peck, a noted itinerant preacher of that day, and asked for support of Peck's efforts to take the gospel to the Indians. McLain's response, if less than charitable, was at least pardonable: "I will give as much as any man, according to my means, to buy powder and lead to kill them all; but I will not give one dollar for all the attempts to Christianize them, as you call it."

CAMP Meeting at Night
A Strange Wilderness Scene

The sights and sounds of the camp meeting presented one of the most unusual spectacles ever witnessed on the American frontier. The camp meeting was a part of a revival movement that swept the frontier of Kentucky, Tennessee, the Carolinas, and Georgia in the early 1800's.

Indescribable screams and wails piercing the summer night attracted the wilderness traveler to the camp ground. As he approached in the dark, he saw scores of lamps and torches dotting a glade or hillside. Approaching the unusual display of lights, which were hanging from trees, poles, and other vantage points, the curious traveler was amazed to find hundreds of men, women, and children gathered in a wilderness clearing. Sometimes a meetinghouse was nearby.

Tents and other crude shelters dotted the clearing, and nearby horses, wagons, and carriages were gathered. At the edge of the clearing a stage had been erected, and from this a preacher delivered a sermon in loud and urgent tones. Several preachers sometimes held forth at the same time, preaching from stumps or other elevations in the clearing. They often preached for hours—or all night—warning sinners to repent.

More remarkable than the preachers was the response of their congregations. Some of the listeners had traveled many miles through the wilderness to attend the camp meeting. They responded to the preaching with weeping, singing, laughing, groaning, and screaming.

The "falling exercise" was one of the more unusual responses. Perhaps with a shrill cry as if in pain, the worshiper fell to the ground as if struck by lightning. Sometimes he remained as still and silent as death. At other times he sobbed uncontrollably or pleaded to God for mercy.

Others attending camp meetings sometimes jerked the head rapidly back and forth, rolled on the ground, ran or danced, barked or howled, or "saw visions."

Presbyterian, Methodist, and Baptist churches were affected by the frontier revival. Many Baptist churches withheld from the camp meetings, however, objecting to the extreme emotional appeal and response of many of these meetings.

TWO Plowboys Sent Forth as Mounted Missionaries

Two young "Bedford plowboys," as they were called, were sent out as home missionaries by the newly organized General Association of Baptists in Virginia. Equipped with stuffed saddlebags, plus overcoats and umbrellas as protection against the weather, the mounted missionaries left Bedford, Virginia, in 1823 to take the Baptist gospel to the frontier.

Only recently called to the ministry, the young men, Jeremiah Jeter and Daniel Witt, were sent on a two-month tour of

Jeremiah B. Jeter

"destitute places" of the state. Their monthly salary was $30 each.

As agents, Jeter and Witt carried on the principal work of the state association. The constitution of the organization stated: "It shall be the entire object of this General Association to propagate the Gosepel and advance the Redeemer's Kingdom throughout the State, by supplying vacant churches with the preached word, and by sending preachers into destitute regions within the limits of the State."

Actually, the General Association was a state convention, but this name was avoided in forming the organization because of some opposition to conventions. Autonomy of local churches and associations was insured by this article in the constitution: "These representatives, when convened, shall in no case interfere with the internal regulations of the churches or Associations, nor shall they pursue any other object than that specified."

The two missionaries were supported by the General Association, and contributions from district associations were voluntary. District associations were not required to make contributions in order to be represented in the state organization.

BORN a Yankee, Raised a Mohawk, Said Leading Georgia Churchman

A man who said he was "born a Yankee and raised a Mohawk Indian" probably baptized more converts and established and strengthened more churches on the Georgia frontier than any other Baptist.

He was Abraham Marshall, a plain son of the frontier with little formal schooling. Yet, he was a member of the Georgia Constitutional Convention in 1789, served in the American Revolution as a soldier and chaplain, was a trustee of the University of Georgia, and for many years was moderator of the Georgia Baptist Association.

For thirty-five years Marshall was pastor of the Kiokee Baptist Church, first Baptist congregation organized in Georgia. Almost from the time he was baptized in the Savannah River until his death nearly fifty years later, Marshall rode the backwoods trails of Georgia, taking the gospel to the frontier settlers.

Abraham was the son of Daniel Marshall, fearless pioneer preacher and patriot. Before moving to Georgia, Daniel was a missionary to the Mohawks, prompting his son to say that he was raised as an Indian.

One of Abraham Marshall's outstanding achievements was the gathering of the First Negro Baptist Church of Georgia near Savannah in 1788. Marshall baptized forty-five converts in constituting the church.

MEETINGHOUSES Reflected Simple Tastes of Baptists

The rugged character and simple tastes of Baptists were reflected in the meetinghouses they built in the 1800's. Scattered from the seaports of the Atlantic to the Mississippi River, most of the meetinghouses were bare and plain.

The Baptist meetinghouse on the frontier was a log cabin, small and crude. Wind whistled through the cracks between the logs, and many had earthen floors. Few had stoves or chimneys, and the women often took foot warmers to services.

Frontier meetinghouses often were located near a prominent

family in the settlement in the hope that this prosperous settler would keep the building in good repair. If the settler did not measure up to expectations and the building were neglected, another meetinghouse might be erected near a more faithful member.

Baptist churches frequently were found on the outskirts of a small town, because the property was given to the church. Sometimes such "generosity" was prompted by the landowner's hope that erection of a church would enhance the value of his property.

Seldom did Baptist congregations of that day spend money for stained glass or other ornamentation. If a church were painted on the outside and whitewashed on the inside, little other embellishment was considered necessary.

Even in the larger churches of the day, carpets and cushions were rare. Pews usually were crude, but in some churches seats could be raised or lowered as the congregation stood for singing, Scripture reading, and prayer. The rising and seating of the congregation during the services was accompanied by the clattering and banging of the wooden seats.

The family pew in some of the larger churches was often an exception to the usual simplicity. These were occupied by wealthier members and often were elaborately furnished to suit the tastes of the owners. Several of these in a church, each finished in distinctive style, gave the place of worship a strange appearance.

YOUNG Baptist Preacher Feared by British Forces

One young Baptist preacher was so feared by the British during the American Revolution that they placed a price of one thousand pounds on his head. Lord Cornwallis, commander of British forces, is said to have "feared the prayers of that godly youth more than the armies of Sumter and Marion."

The youth was Richard Furman, later to serve as pastor of

the First Baptist Church of Charleston, South Carolina, for thirty-eight years. Furman's list of accomplishments during a long life of devotion to his country and his faith is impressive. A few highlights follow:

- *Delegate to the South Carolina Constitutional Convention in 1790. He was a leader in the fight for religious freedom.*
- *Elected first president of the Triennial Convention when it was formed in 1814.*
- *Helped to organize South Carolina Baptists into the first state Baptist convention in 1821.*

Richard Furman

Educated at home by his father, Furman was ordained at nineteen and became known as the "boy evangelist." Once a sheriff refused to allow young Furman to preach at the county courthouse because he was not a member of the clergy of the established church. But after the eloquent young Baptist had preached in the open, he was never again denied use of the building.

WOODS Were Full of Baptists On the American Frontier

The woods of the American frontier around 1800 were full of Baptists. The hardy, freedom-loving Baptists were well suited for the rugged life of the frontier.

Having fought a stubborn fight for liberty in Virginia and other coastal states and secured freedom of worship under the newly-adopted Constitution, many Baptists moved westward toward the Mississippi. Cheap land, their need to breathe the air of freedom, and their own rugged character turned Baptists toward the frontier.

Liberty-loving Baptists had not always found life to their liking in the coastal states. In New England, Virginia, and elsewhere, they were often persecuted by the established church. Repeatedly they had been forced to fight for the right to worship God as they saw fit.

The cheap lands of the frontier appealed to Baptists of the day because, as a group, they were not wealthy. Most of them were farmers and merchants. Many were impoverished by the Revolutionary War, in which Baptists fought almost to a man for the cause of liberty.

The leveling influence of the frontier, where men met each other as equals, also appealed to the democratic Baptists. Few of them had become plantation owners, and the social life of Virginia and New England had little appeal to them.

A pioneer home.

The hardy traveling Baptist preacher also played a major role in the growth of Baptists on the frontier. Most frontier preachers were self-supporting. They handled the rifle and ax during the week and the Word of God on Sunday. They often spent weeks on the wilderness trail, taking the Baptist message by foot and by horseback to the remote cabins of the frontier.

One of the early Baptist frontier preachers was Squire Boone, brother of Daniel Boone. Like Daniel Boone, the famous hunter and trailblazer, Squire Boone and other frontier Baptists were a courageous band who loved liberty and were not afraid to fight if necessary to win it or defend it.

LIKE Daniel Boone, Baptist Preacher Also Left His Mark

Daniel Boone left his mark on the wilderness frontier by blazing trails. John Taylor, a Baptist preacher of the same era, also left his mark—Baptist churches.

A pioneer preacher who saw more of the Virginia and Kentucky frontier than many explorers and trappers, John Taylor was untiring in his efforts to spread the gospel on the frontier. He probably rode more miles and preached more sermons than any other pioneer preacher in Kentucky. Hostile Indians, the trackless wilderness, frozen and flooded streams, mud, cold, rain—nothing stopped John Taylor in his self-appointed mission to preach to settlers in the remote cabins of the wilderness.

Not long after the fearless evangelist arrived in Kentucky, with all his worldly goods loaded on three wagons, he became the messenger for the first revival in the state. It began in Taylor's cabin in the wilderness, which had the earth for a floor. It ended with the formation of another Baptist church.

Baptist churches that John Taylor established in Kentucky included Corn Creek, Clear Creek, Great Crossing, Boone's Creek, Bullittsburg, and Buck Run.

The backwoods preacher never forgot one preaching tour in the mountains of Virginia in the dead of winter. Coming to an icy stream with his two horses, Taylor attempted to cross a crude bridge which collapsed. After gaining the other side, he dismounted and walked to keep from freezing in his drenched clothes.

His nervous mounts broke away and raced across the snow. After chasing the horses for several miles, he finally caught them at the edge of another stream. Since there was no bridge at all at this stream, there was no choice for the traveler but to take another icy bath and swim across.

He finally reached a settler's cabin after dark, nearly frozen and his hands and arms numb and swollen. Dazed for several days by his ordeal, the evangelist broke out in a scaly rash which covered most of his body. Taylor bore to his grave the scars of the rash and the memory of his most hazardous preaching tour.

SINGLE Word Led Baptists To Form New Bible Society

A single word called 290 delegates from twenty-three states to Philadelphia in 1837 to organize the American and Foreign Bible Society. The one word—always of singular importance to Baptists—was "baptize."

Baptists had supported the American Bible Society since it was formed in 1816. The society in turn had printed and circulated the Scriptures in many languages translated by the missionaries of various denominations.

A leading Baptist translator was Adoniram Judson, missionary to Burma. Judson was always careful to translate words related to baptism as the equivalent of "immerse" or "dip."

When Baptists asked the American Bible Society to aid in printing a Bengali version of the Scriptures based on Judson's translations, there was delay. Then the society announced a new policy. It could promote only such versions of the Bible as all denominations represented in the society could consistently use and circulate. Some denominations objected to Baptist insistence on translating "baptize" to mean immerse.

Rather than be untrue to their understanding of the Scriptures, Baptists decided to go their own way and formed the American and Foreign Bible Society.

HOME Mission Society Older Than Convention

Six years before the Southern Baptist Convention was formed, the Southern Baptist Home Mission Society was organized in Columbus, Mississippi, in 1839.

Since the formation of the American Baptist Home Mission Society in 1832, many Baptists in the South had been displeased with the failure of that agency to send home missionaries to Southern states. They felt that Southern churches were giving their money to support mission work in the North while their own states were neglected.

In 1835, American Baptists did not have a single missionary in Kentucky, Louisiana, Alabama, or Florida, and only one in Mississippi. By contrast, sixteen missionaries served in Michigan.

Southern Baptists further argued that there was only one home missionary for every 400,000 souls in the South, while there was one missionary for every 4,000 persons in Northern states such as Illinois and Indiana.

Formation of the Home Mission Society marked the beginning of organized efforts by Southern Baptists to withdraw from the Baptist General Convention, dominated by Northern interests, and to chart their own course.

WITH a Gold Watch and Little Money, Alabama Baptists Formed a Convention

With a treasury that included $362.67, a gold watch, a pair of socks, two boxes of clothing, and other provisions, the Alabama Baptist Convention was formed in 1823.

Although the treasury was not impressive by modern standards, Alabama Baptists made ambitious plans. Gifts were designated for ministry to the Indians and for promotion of missions,

Bible distribution, ministerial education, and subscriptions.

Fifteen delegates from missionary societies met at Salem Church near Greensboro to draw up a constitution and to form the state convention. The societies originally were formed by Luther Rice, who helped to organize Baptists for the support of foreign missions.

Alabama was the fourth state to form a state Baptist convention. First was South Carolina in 1821, followed by Georgia and Virginia.

A BITTER Foe of Baptists Was Alexander Campbell

Just as one man, Luther Rice, helped to unite Baptists to support missions, another man rose up to divide the struggling denomination. Baptists in America have seldom faced a more bitter foe than Alexander Campbell.

Campbell was baptized in 1812 and at one time was pastor of a Baptist church. But he soon came to oppose almost everything that Baptists stood for.

In addition to their belief that baptism is essential to salvation, followers of Campbell were on the opposite side of the fence from Baptists on many other issues. They opposed missions, ministerial education, Bible and tract societies, Sunday schools, church covenants, ordination, and other so-called "man made" institutions.

For years Campbellism created dissension and strife in Baptist churches from Georgia to Pennsylvania. Kentucky was hard hit, losing perhaps 10,000 members to Campbellism in a few years. Tennessee, Georgia, Virginia, and North Carolina also suffered heavy losses.

Loss of membership was only one of the hurts suffered by Baptists. Campbellism divided churches, weakened the budding mission movement, and drained off energies in quarreling and bickering that could have been put to better use.

Campbell's avowed purpose was to unite all denominations in one belief common with his own. He succeeded only in launching another religious group.

FOLLY for Men to Attempt Work of Holy Spirit, Declared Early Foes of Foreign Mission Program

No sooner were Baptists in America organized for the support of a foreign mission program than an anti-mission movement sprang up to oppose the mission effort. Opposition to missions was especially strong on the frontier.

Some who opposed foreign missions pointed out that it was folly to send out missionaries "to do the work of the Holy Spirit." Others declared that they favored foreign missions but were opposed to a foreign mission board.

Democratic Baptists feared the central power of a mission board, charging that it was contrary to the cherished Baptist principle of the autonomy of the local church. Frugal Baptists also were reluctant to invest heavily in this costly venture. Luther Rice and other leaders of the mission movement conducted extensive fund-raising campaigns, and anti-mission Baptists tired of this drain on the finances of the churches.

Many farmer-preachers served their frontier churches with little or no pay, and some were suspicious of the salaried representatives of the mission program.

"Judas was a lover of money, and money and power is the watchword of the whole missionary scheme," charged John Taylor, a frontier preacher in Kentucky and Virginia. "The very many modes and artful measures of these great men to get money are disgustful to common modesty. They begin with missionary societies, then create Female Societies, Cent Societies, Mite Societies, Children Societies, and even Negro Societies. Their shameful cravings are insatiable."

Another bitter foe of foreign missions was Daniel Parker, a backwoods preacher reared in poverty in Georgia.

"It makes me shudder," Parker wrote, "to think that I am the first to draw the sword against this error or to shoot at it and spare no arrows. The Mission Board plans to take over government of the ministry and usurp the authority of Christ over his Church.

"The society calls men to preach, assigns them to fields, and holds education necessary for the gospel ministry—all of which usurp the work of God. The mission program has neither precept nor example to justify it within the two lids of the Bible."

Opponents of the foreign mission program and other united efforts of Baptists were soon to bow to progress, however. Three decades after Baptists were organized to support two foreign missionaries sent out by another denomination, both Northern and Southern Baptists had mission programs.

CHURCHES Need Bible Only, Said Some Frontier Baptists

The suspicion with which some frontier Baptist churches regarded all outsiders, and anything that could not be found "within the two lids of the Bible," is reflected in this excerpt from an early Missouri Baptist confession of faith.

"We believe that everything necessary for the instruction and good discipline of the church is recorded in the Holy Scriptures, and should be strictly attended to—at the same time avoiding every tradition and invention of men, such as the Sunday-school union, Bible society, tract societies of all kinds, rag societies, temperance societies, and what is generally known by the Baptist board of foreign missions, home missions, and all ecclesiastical schools for the instruction of preachers, with all other inventions of men, under the head of religion, which the New Testament does not warrant. And this association does hereby declare that she will not hold any member in fellowship who will invite or allow preachers or tutors of the above societies into their houses after they are known to them; for we believe those who do it are partakers of their evil deeds. The foregoing articles are not to be so construed as to say, we forbid our members from entertaining strangers and travelers; nor to say we are opposed to learning; those we reject are only to be rejected in their public character, as not being able ministers of the New Testament."

MONEY No Problem For Preacher—He Had None

How to manage his money was one problem that the Baptist preacher of an earlier time did not have. Most congregations protected their pastors from the evils of filthy lucre by keeping them poor.

Many churches paid their preachers little or nothing for their services. For this reason most Baptist preachers, particularly those on the frontier, were self-supporting.

Some congregations agreed to pay their pastors a certain sum each year, but often these pledges went unpaid. Frontier preachers sometimes had as many as four churches in their charge, preaching at each once a month. Their support from these churches usually was slight.

John Mason Peck, an outstanding itinerant Baptist preacher, conducted worship services 174 times one year at widely-separated points along the Mississippi River frontier. For his services he received a total of $61.95.

To these frontier evangelists, the preachers in the larger coastal towns seemed to be men of wealth. Pastors of some of the larger churches received as much as $500 a year and a parsonage. Their call often was on an annual basis, however, and their tenure sometimes was uncertain.

Frequently the frontier preacher was paid in salt, corn, wheat, flour, sugar, tallow—and whiskey. The only money some received was in fees and gifts for officiating at marriages and funerals.

The reluctance of Baptists to pay their preachers a salary probably grew out of their dislike for the "hired clergy" of the established church. Baptists of colonial days strongly opposed taxation for the support of these ministers.

FIRST Baptist Church Formed At "The Devil's Headquarters"

Traveling preachers on the Mississippi River valley frontier let nothing stop them in their efforts to spread the gospel. One hardy band invaded the "devil's headquarters" itself and there planted a Baptist church.

Three Baptist evangelists arrived at a small settlement near the river in the summer of 1839. They approached a hotel keeper and asked him about the chances of conducting a meeting.

"To be candid, I would say a very poor chance," the hotel keeper replied. "Presbyterians and Methodists have tried and failed—the Baptists need not try at all. In fact, this town is called 'The Devil's Headquarters.' "

The preachers agreed that this was just the kind of town they were looking for and went to work. A small log cabin served as the local courthouse. They swept and cleaned the cabin and announced their meeting.

Twelve persons attended the first meeting. But at the second, the tiny cabin was crowded. In a few days the crowds were so large that the meeting was moved to a nearby grove.

Many hearers approached the mourner's bench, seeking salvation. The converts who were baptized formed the nucleus of the First Baptist Church at "The Devil's Headquarters."

FRONTIER Baptists Soon Saw Evils of Beverage Alcohol

Although frontier Baptist preachers sometimes received a part of their salary in whiskey, and drinking was common among both pastors and congregations, Baptists soon saw the evils of beverage alcohol.

One hundred years ago, an association in Missouri passed the following resolution against the sale and use of intoxicants and encouraged an annual temperance sermon.

"*Whereas,* there is a tendency among some of our good people to countenance the sale of intoxicating liquors and advocate a moderate use of the same; and, *whereas,* all the drunkards of the land come from the ranks of the moderate dram-drinkers; and, *whereas,* it is our opinion that the moderate dram-drinker is leading many of the most prominent young men of our country into the haunts of drunkenness, degradation and ruin; we therefore recommend:

"That each of our church members be admonished to abstain from the use and discourage the sale of intoxicating liquors, except strictly for medical use, and on the recommendation of their family physician.

"That each of our ministers be requested to preach at least once a year to their churches on the subject of intemperance."

The Fight Between Brothers

CHURCH of One Thousand Was Born Full-Grown

A church of one thousand members was born full-grown when the First African Baptist Church of Richmond, Virginia, was formed in 1841.

Members of the church, both free and slave, formerly belonged to the First Baptist Church of Richmond and occupied the old First Baptist Church building. White members of the church, totaling almost 400, moved to a new building.

For years slaves worshiped with their masters in the First Baptist Church and were baptized into membership by the pastor. By 1825, two-thirds of the membership was black.

During and following the Civil War, most of the blacks who had been members of Southern Baptist churches left to form churches of their own.

LONG Before Civil War Virginia Baptists Decried Slavery

Almost three-quarters of a century before slavery divided the nation, Baptists of Virginia declared slaveholding a violent deprivation of human rights.

In 1789, Baptists in Virginia petitioned their fellow Baptists "to make use of every legal measure to extirpate this horrid evil from the land; and pray Almighty God that our honorable Legislature may have it in their power to proclaim the great

Jubilee, consistent with the principles of good policy."

Many Baptist slave owners did not defend the practice—even deplored it—but felt helpless to abolish a system they had inherited. Some wanted to free their slaves but believed that such a move would not be in the best interest of the slaves. With few exceptions, the slaves were ignorant and unskilled. Many in the South believed that the slaves would be helpless without their masters.

Other Baptists defended slavery, insisting that the Bible condoned it. They argued that Christians should hold their slaves and treat them with mercy and kindness.

Slaves were brought to America by the Dutch in 1619—before the Pilgrims landed at Plymouth Rock.

SOUTHERN Baptists Showed Early Concern for Slaves

Although slavery was the major issue which divided Baptists of the North and South, Southern Baptists immediately expressed concern for the welfare of slaves.

At the second meeting of the Southern Baptist Convention, at Richmond, Virginia, in 1846, this resolution was passed: "That in view of the present conditions of the African race, and in view of the indications of Divine Providence toward that portion of the great family of fallen men, we feel that a solemn obligation rests not only upon the Convention, but upon all Christians, to furnish them with the gospel and a suitable Christian ministry."

Southern Baptists withdrew from the Triennial Convention to form their own convention after officials of the Triennial Convention ruled that they could not appoint a slaveholder as a missionary.

Both the Foreign Mission Board and the Home Mission Board gave encouraging reports at the second meeting of the Southern Baptist Convention. The Home Mission Board announced it had hired six missionaries to begin work on the home field.

SLAVEHOLDING Was the Issue That Finally Divided Baptists

A denomination that could not be split by doctrinal disputes, internal strife, and other differences finally was broken by the same issue that plunged the nation into civil war—slavery.

Southern Baptists meet to form new convention.

Although other factors contributed to the rift between Northern and Southern Baptists—just as other factors led to civil war—the central issue in both divisions was slavery.

The break for Baptists came when 300 delegates from eight Southern states and the District of Columbia met at Augusta, Georgia, May 8-11, 1845, to form the Southern Baptist Convention.

Southern Baptists withdrew from the Baptist General Convention after its Home Mission Society announced that it would not appoint a slaveholder as a missionary. In making the announcement, Convention executives said, "One thing is certain, we can never be a party to any arrangement which would imply approbation of slavery."

Until that time the Convention had carefully maintained a position of neutrality on the slavery question.

During the thirty-one years that Northern and Southern Baptists worked together in the old Triennial Convention, only once did the Convention meet south of Washington. Because of the distance and expense, churches of the South were poorly represented at those sessions.

NORTHERN, Southern Conventions Had Similar Mission Objectives

Although Baptists of the South believed that they had no other choice than to withdraw from their Northern brethren in 1845, the stated purpose of the Southern Baptist Convention was almost identical with that of the parent convention in the North.

The Southern Baptist Convention was formed at Augusta, Georgia, "for eliciting, combining and directing energies of the whole denomination for the propagation of the gospel."

When "The General Missionary Convention of the Baptist Denomination in the United States for Foreign Missions" was formed at Philadelphia in 1814, its purpose was to direct "the energies of the whole denomination in one sacred effort for sending the glad tidings of salvation to the heathen, and to nations destitute of pure gospel light."

Thus, it was a desire to proclaim the gospel, particularly on mission fields, that led to the formation of both conventions.

Some 300 delegates from Virginia, Maryland, North Carolina, South Carolina, Georgia, Alabama, Louisiana, Kentucky, and the District of Columbia met at Augusta to form the Southern Baptist Convention. Two other states were represented by letter.

W. B. Johnson

W. B. Johnson of South Carolina, former president of the Baptist General Convention, was elected first president of the Southern Baptist Convention.

Two boards of managers were formed, one for foreign missions and the other for domestic missions.

Delegates decided to form a convention that would support the entire range of missionary and educational work under one organization, rather than form separate societies for each interest, as the Baptist General Convention had done.

SBC a Blessing in Disguise, North and South Soon Agreed

Baptists of both the North and South soon realized that the formation of the Southern Baptist Convention, born out of strife, was a blessing in disguise.

Leaders on both sides regretted the dissension which led to the new convention. Many Baptists in the South believed the action premature when the Southern Baptist Convention was formed. Later it was generally agreed that the break was inevitable. Rather than diminishing, differences between North and South mounted.

Slaveholding was the pivotal issue which brought on the division, but that was not the only issue. There were differences in culture, economics, morality, and religious fervor which divided the country, as well as Baptists.

At least ten years before the Southern Baptist Convention was formed, Baptists of the South were dissatisfied with home mission efforts in the South by the Baptist General Convention. They believed they were being discriminated against in favor of northern and eastern states.

With two conventions, Baptists could more effectively serve needs at home and abroad. As westward expansion continued, needs in the West multiplied. Two home mission boards were able to meet those needs better than one.

During the first year of the Southern Baptist Convention, home and foreign mission boards received gifts totaling more than $30,000. This was evidence that a convention free of dissension and strife could work more effectively.

To hold Baptists in the North and South together, it was soon agreed, was no justification for holding up the spread of the gospel at home and abroad.

SCRIPTURES Used to Defend Both Sides of Slavery Issue

In good Baptist tradition, both exponents and opponents of slavery used the Bible to defend their position.

Abolitionists insisted that slavery was against all principles of Christianity, pointing out that Christ came to make all men "free indeed." Slaveholders, on the other hand, argued that the

Bible had nothing to say against slavery, and that Negroes owed their salvation to the fact that they were brought to America where they heard the gospel.

Slavery was long a knotty problem for Baptists. In 1789, John Leland led Virginia Baptists to petition the General Assembly to outlaw slavery in the state. Baptist associations in many Southern states adopted resolutions opposing the buying and selling of slaves.

Although abolitionists were strongest in the North, and most slaveholders lived in the South, feeling over the question was sharply divided in all sections, even before the Civil War.

Recognizing slavery as an explosive issue, Baptists of the North generally took a moderate stand. When the Triennial Convention met in Philadelphia in 1844, only eighty of the 460 delegates were from the South. Yet, the Convention adopted a neutral position on the slavery question.

Abolitionists were largely responsible for the changing attitude toward slavery after 1840, inflaming feelings in both the North and South. Many slaveholders had inherited their slaves and favored freeing them gradually. They rebelled only against forced and sudden emancipation—much as their descendants would rebel against forced racial integration of public schools one hundred years later.

Thousands of slaves were members of white Baptist churches before the Civil War. They worshiped with whites, were baptized by the same pastor, and had a voice in the government of their church.

RESOLUTION Asking Prayer For Baptist Editors Failed

Editors may have a way with words, but they do not always have the last word.

When the Southern Baptist Convention met in Richmond, Virginia, in 1859, the controversy over Landmarkism was raging.

Baptist papers of the day were filled with news and opinions regarding the conflict between J. R. Graves and R. B. C. Howell. Convention proceedings were interrupted by a brother offering a resolution to the effect that everyone should pray for the Baptist editors.

J. R. Graves

The Convention president, Richard Fuller, was not a skilled parliamentarian. Not sure how he should dispose of the resolution, Fuller responded, "Well, now, my dear brother, we will think about this matter."

The Convention broke up in laughter over the presiding officer's discomfort, and the motion to pray for Baptist editors failed to carry.

BIBLES Instead of Bullets

While the Civil War raged, churches and Sunday Schools of the South tried to carry on. Because the Southern Baptist Convention did not establish a publication board when it was formed in 1845, there was a shortage of Bibles and other literature in the South.

Under a flag of truce, the American Bible Society sent 25,000 New Testaments to Greenville, South Carolina, for distribution and use in the Sunday Schools of the South.

SOUTHERN Baptist Churches Seized by Northern Baptists

Not only was the South invaded by armies of the North during the Civil War, but some Southern Baptist churches found themselves invaded by the American Baptist Home Mission Society.

In 1863 the Home Mission Society of New York applied to the War Department for authority to seize abandoned Southern Baptist meetinghouses in areas overrun by Union troops. The War Department not only granted the request but ordered that "all houses of worship belonging to the Baptist Churches South," where there was no officiating minister, be turned over to the American Baptist Home Mission Society. Pastors of many churches in the South had left to serve with Confederate forces as chaplains and in other capacities.

The stated purpose of Northern Baptists was to protect Baptist property in the South from marauders and to preserve it for future Baptist use. While the motive of Baptists in the North may have been unselfish, there were many abuses of the plan. Some churches still occupied by Southern Baptists were seized by force. Such action stirred much indignation among Southern Baptists and served to further divide the two conventions.

STONEWALL Jackson's Death Shocked Southern Baptists

When "Stonewall" Jackson was struck down during the Civil War, Southern Baptists were quick to recognize that the South had lost a great leader.

Returning to Augusta, Georgia, where the Convention had been formed in 1845, the Convention of 1863 passed the following resolution: "That we have just heard with unutterable grief of the death of that noble Christian warrior, Lieut. Gen. T. J. Jackson; that we thank God for the good he has achieved, and the glorious example he has left us, and pray that we may all learn to trust, as he trusted, in the Lord alone."

Jackson was shot by his own men in a tragic accident during the fighting at Chancellorsville, Virginia, in May, 1863.

BROTHERS' War Divided Many Baptist Families

The "brothers' war" of 1861-65 divided many families. One Tennessee Baptist preacher who was a Union sympathizer found that most of his family "by blood and by marriage" was on the other side.

The preacher's son enlisted as a Confederate soldier. Although they were on opposite sides, father and son kept up a loving correspondence until the boy was killed in action.

Many Tennesseans did not welcome this Union sympathizer in their midst. The preacher suffered the supreme slander when a newspaper published a report that he had pronounced a curse on his son and expressed the wish that the boy might be killed in the first battle.

Slander was not the only ill suffered by the father. A fellow townsman announced that he would head any group that would undertake to hang the Union sympathizer. The Baptist made a practice of leaving a back window and shutter open before retiring, so he could escape in the event an attempt were made on his life during the night.

CHURCHES Turned Steeple Bells Into Cannons for Confederacy

As the South rallied to the cause of the Confederacy, Christians were called upon, not to beat their swords into plowshares, but to melt their church bells into cannons.

The following notice appeared in one of the state Baptist papers in 1862.

"The Confederate States solicit the use of bells for the

purpose of providing light artillery for the war. Those who are willing to devote their bells to this patriotic purpose will receive receipts for them, and the bells will be replaced, if required, at the end of the war, or they will be purchased at their fair prices. Persons and congregations placing their bells at the service of the Government are requested to send a statement of the fact, with a description and weight of the bell, to the chairman of the bureau of ordnance, at Richmond, for record in the war department. The Government will pay all charges of transportation and promptly return receipts.

"Let our church bells, throughout the whole Confederacy, be brought down from our steeples and moulded into cannon."

Less than six decades later, the same Baptist paper deplored the fact that the Germans were reported to have converted 70,000 church bells into munitions of war to fight the Allies during World War I. Now bells that had called the people to worship, it was noted, would call the German people to mourning.

CHAPLAIN Whose Robe Was Stolen Told, "Send Coat and Boots Also"

Many Southern Baptist pastors served bravely and well as chaplains in the armies of the Confederacy during the Civil War.

Usually these chaplains were held in high esteem by the officers and men of the Confederacy. When Robert E. Lee was told that the chaplains were praying for his welfare, the godly general replied, "I can only say that I am nothing but a poor sinner, trusting in Christ alone for salvation, and need all of the prayers they can offer for me."

Sometimes, however, the chaplains were the targets of good-humored teasing and practical jokes. When one chaplain advertised in a Richmond, Virginia, newspaper for the return of a buffalo robe that he said had been stolen from him, the following response later appeared in the same paper.

"I was inexpressibly shocked to learn that the temporary loan of your buffalo robe, blankets, shawl, and pillow should

have given you such inconvenience. Had I known that these articles belonged to a chaplain, the sacred package should have remained inviolate.

"We are, all of us, exceedingly anxious for you to change your field of labor to this army, where the duties of chaplains are much lighter than they could possibly be anywhere else. Here they devote themselves to trading horses and collecting table delicacies.

"I am now patiently waiting for your coat and boots, which I presume you will send to me, in accordance with the following injunction: 'If any man take away thy coat, let him have thy cloak also' (Matt. 5:40).

"For the regulation of the amount of baggage which a chaplain in the army should carry, we refer you to the following: 'Provide . . . neither two coats; neither shoes, nor yet staves' (Matt. 10:9-10).

"Anything you may have in excess of the above allowance will be respectfully received by me."

THE MAN WHO STOLE YOUR BUFFALO ROBE

FEW Churches Suffered More Than First Baptist, Nashville

Few churches were hit harder by the ravages of civil war than the First Baptist Church of Nashville, Tennessee.

With the outbreak of war in 1861, many Southerners thought the gallant soldiers of the Confederacy would score an early victory. Imagine the shock of Nashvillians early in 1862 when word came that Fort Donelson had fallen and Federal troops were marching on Nashville.

R. B. C. Howell, the second man to serve as president of the Southern Baptist Convention and pastor of Nashville's First Baptist, tried to conduct Sunday morning worship services the day news arrived that Confederate defenders were in retreat. But as one member after another hurriedly left the congregation, he dismissed the services with prayer.

A few months after Federal troops seized the city, the military governor of Tennessee ordered Howell and other ministers to appear before him. He demanded that they take an oath of loyalty to the United States Government. When Howell and others refused, they were marched off to jail at bayonet point.

Shortly after his imprisonment, Howell became ill. Although he was jailed for almost two months and his recovery from illness was slow, he was not allowed visits from members of his flock.

When he was at last released, Howell was warned that he would be under strict military surveillance at all times. Just what the military governor and Federal troops feared in the pastor is unclear.

After Union forces had been in Nashville almost a year, they seized the First Baptist Church building and converted it into a hospital in January, 1863. Soldiers piled pews and other church furniture in the yard, leaving deacons the task of storing the property at church expense.

While the church was without a building, the congregation worshiped at the Christian Church and in a theater. Ironically, a few years before the Christian Church offered the use of its building, the Baptists had voted not to allow that church to use its building while the Christian Church was being repaired. Later the Baptists condemned as a place of worldly amusement the theater they had used.

First Baptist, Nashville, was homeless for more than two years. When at last they were allowed to return to their building, they found it a shambles. The Federal Government paid the church $5,000 for the "loan" of its property, but the cost to the church for remodeling was more than twice that sum.

FIGHT for Religious Freedom Renewed Following Civil War

The fight for religious freedom, which Baptists thought had been secured by the First Amendment to the Constitution, had to be renewed at the close of the Civil War.

Some states adopted a "test oath" which required those who

had sided with the Confederacy to sign a pledge of loyalty to the Union. Preachers were required to sign the oath before they were allowed to preach. Baptists opposed this oath, declaring that it was in violation of the First Amendment.

The oath adopted in Missouri read: "no person shall . . . be competent as a bishop, priest, deacon, minister, elder, or other clergyman of any religious persuasion, sect, or denomination, to teach, or preach, or solemnize marriages, unless such person shall have first taken, subscribed and filed said oath."

Punishment for violation of the oath was "by fine not less than five hundred dollars, or by imprisonment in the county jail not less than six months, or by both such fine and imprisonment; and whoever shall take said oath falsely, by swearing or by affirmation, shall, on conviction thereof, be adjudged guilty of perjury, and be punished by imprisonment in the penitentiary not less than two years."

Many Baptists in Missouri were persecuted under the oath until it was found unconstitutional by the Supreme Court in 1867.

PREACHER Pistol-whipped For Violating Oath

A Baptist preacher in Missouri was dragged from his home at midnight, pistol-whipped and beaten, and warned to leave the county because he refused to sign a "test oath."

Following the Civil War, Missouri adopted the oath, which required that preachers sign a pledge of loyalty to the Union before preaching. Baptists opposed the oath as a violation of the First Amendment to the Constitution, which insured freedom of worship.

A mob of about fifteen men first broke up the meeting where the minister was preaching. Then that night the mob came to the preacher's home and seized him.

"If you intend to kill me," the preacher pleaded, "do it

here and do not take me away where friends cannot find my body."

His captors then dragged the minister to a nearby woods where they beat him with pistols and sticks. He was given two days to leave the county.

The preacher immediately sold his little farm and moved to another part of the state. He did not recover from his severe beating for several weeks.

SOUTHERN Churches Lost Blacks After Civil War

Although the Southern Baptist Convention continued to grow during the Reconstruction, the Civil War had taken its toll. The annual rate of growth following the war was less than half the growth rate from the launching of the Convention in 1845 until 1860.

In addition to war losses, Southern Baptist churches lost many former slaves who had been members. It is estimated that 400,000 former slaves left Southern Baptist churches during this period to join other churches or to form churches of their own.

This exodus from Southern Baptist churches was encouraged by Northern Baptist missionaries in the South, as well as by Union forces stationed in the South. The blacks themselves regarded this move to establish their own churches as another expression of their newfound freedom.

Although some Southern Baptists believed that the former slaves were not ready to form their own churches, churches in the South generally supported the move. Some Southern Baptist churches gave up their buildings to the blacks, and others offered financial aid and other assistance.

Until the Civil War, slaves were baptized into Baptist churches and worshiped there with their masters for generations.

SUNDAY School Board Fought Competition from the North

Following the Civil War, Northern Baptists apparently regarded the conquered South as "their" territory. Northern Baptists sent more than 100 missionaries into Southern states and, with the help of the War Department, even seized some Southern Baptist churches and other property.

In addition, the American Baptist Publication Society attempted to swallow up the Sunday School Board of the Southern Baptist Convention. In 1896, the North's publication society made a remarkable proposition to James M. Frost, pioneer leader of the infant Sunday School Board. It was proposed that Northern Baptists print Sunday School Board literature, distribute it to Southern Baptist churches, and pay the Sunday School Board half the profits.

When Frost answered that the Sunday School Board could not agree to such a proposal and maintain its integrity, the American Baptist Publication Society stepped up its efforts to capture the Sunday School literature market in the South. It cut literature prices, established branch publication offices in the South, and made public attacks on the Sunday School Board.

As was the case in the home mission controversy between Northern and Southern Baptists, Southern Baptists did not take long to decide where their loyalties lay. Within a decade after the Sunday School Board was established in 1891, it had become one of the Convention's strongest agencies.

NORTHERN Baptists Saw South as Mission Field

Before Baptists in the South withdrew from the Baptist General Convention, one of their complaints was a lack of missionaries at work in Southern states. During and following the Civil War, however, Baptists of the North showed a sudden interest in the South as a mission field.

Missionaries of the American Baptist Home Mission Society moved into the South close on the heels of advancing Union armies. By 1865 there were sixty missionaries from the North working in twelve Southern states.

During the Reconstruction period, Southern Baptists became alarmed at the number of Northern Baptist missionaries at work in the South. They petitioned Baptists of the North, asking that missionaries in Southern states either be appointed or approved by a Southern agency.

This bid the North refused. They continued to send missionaries into Southern states to work with whites, blacks, and Indians. They bypassed the Southern Baptist Convention to work directly with Southern states.

Toward the end of Reconstruction, Northern Baptists had more than 100 missionaries in the South, while Southern Baptists had less than half that number on the field. Resources of Southern Baptists continued to dwindle. Some Baptists began to question whether the Southern Baptist Convention even needed an agency for home missions.

Before the turn of the century, however, Southern Baptists had rallied to the cause of home missions. The Convention's Home Mission Board was firmly established and would soon extend its work throughout the United States.

III

The Pangs of Growth

GENIUS of Luther Rice Behind Two Baptist Papers

The organizing genius of Luther Rice, father of the foreign mission program of Baptists in America, launched two of the earliest Baptist newspapers.

The Religious Herald was first published in Richmond, Virginia, in 1828. In an introductory statement to readers, the editor said that the purpose of the paper was to print essays on Baptist doctrine, progress reports of home and foreign missions, explanatory remarks on difficult passages of Scripture, exposures of conditions hurtful to society, and sketches on biography, literature, and politics.

The Religious Herald was a successor to the *Evangelical Inquirer,* which in turn was a local successor to the *Latter Day Luminary*. Rice launched the *Luminary* in 1816, shortly after he returned from the mission field. He hoped to use the *Luminary,* published in Washington, to rally Baptists to the support of foreign missions.

The Columbian Star and Christian Index, first published under this title in Philadelphia in 1829, also bore Rice's imprint. First published as *The Columbian Star* in Washington in 1822, *Christian Index* was added to the title to make clear the religious character of the paper. The paper was named after Columbian College, also founded in Washington by Rice.

The purpose of *The Columbian Star and Christian Index* was to provide "missionary and other religious intelligence, as

well as a medium for inculcating sound theological doctrines and pure moral concepts."

The Religious Herald survives today as the state paper of Virginia Baptists. *The Christian Index* is the state Baptist paper of Georgia.

NORTH America for Christ Was Home Missions Slogan

With the slogan "North America for Christ," the American Baptist Home Mission Society was formed in New York in 1832.

As Luther Rice was the father of the foreign mission program, launched in 1814 with the formation of the Triennial Convention, so John Mason Peck was the father of home missions. A tireless frontier missionary with the courage of a Daniel Boone, Peck labored in the West for years.

Work of the home society was concentrated along the Mississippi River valley, but included other regions as well as Canada. The society was formed with the blessings of the Triennial Convention, which was free to concentrate its energies on foreign missions.

Peck was appointed by the Triennial Convention as a domestic missionary to the Missouri Territory in 1817. He continued to labor in the West, even after the convention withdrew support.

The Massachusetts Baptist Missionary Society hired Peck as a missionary to the West in 1822 at a salary of $5 a week. Later he was joined in his labors by Jonathan Going. Going was named the first secretary of the Home Mission Society.

SOUTHERN Baptists Wished to Avoid "Embarrassment" of Book Publication

With the formation of the Southern Baptist Convention in 1845, there was strong sentiment for also establishing a publication society. A year later, however, the Convention rejected a proposal to establish boards of publication and Bible distribution. Instead, it adopted this resolution: "That this Convention does not deem it advisable to embarrass itself with an enterprise for the publication and sale of books."

The present Sunday School Board was not established until

1891. During a recent year of operation, the Board's Program of Broadman Publishing "embarrassed itself" by introducing 428 new products, including 66 books, with sales totaling $6,000,000.

HUSBAND Shot Preacher For Baptizing His Wife

To Baptists of a hundred years ago, persecution was not unusual. But one Baptist preacher's suffering was out of the ordinary. He was shot by an irate husband for baptizing the man's wife.

The preacher, John Tanner, was shot in the leg with buckshot from a large horseman's pistol. His assailant, stepping out of hiding to fire at close range, ambushed the preacher.

A physician removed seventeen buckshot from the preacher's leg. He was confined for several weeks while recovering but did not press charges. His assailant, a supporter of the state church, was a leading persecutor of Baptists in the area.

Several years before the shooting, Tanner had been arrested for preaching without a license from the state church of Virginia. He was accused of "disturbing the peace"—the usual charge made against Baptist preachers who opposed the state church.

HOT Stove and Hot Pepper Can Break Up a Meeting

Pastors and congregations took their religion seriously in the nineteenth century, and sometimes churches and denominations bitterly opposed one another.

One traveling Baptist evangelist, holding a revival in New York, exposed what he regarded as the errors of the Universalists. When he noted that attendance and interest increased, he continued his attack on that group.

His opponents were not without defense, however. One winter evening as the evangelist preached to a packed house, someone threw a sackful of cayenne pepper on the meetinghouse stove. As fumes filled the house, the congregation was seized with spasms of sneezing, coughing, and gasping for breath. Doors and windows were immediately thrown open and fresh air let in before the preacher could continue.

The evangelist claimed the final victory. He reported 100 baptisms during the protracted meeting.

BAPTISMS at Midnight Awakened Sleeping City

Baptists of another day not only openly opposed infant baptism and sprinkling, but made much of their own distinctive mode of baptism. It was not unusual for an evangelist to lead a processional through the streets of a town to a nearby river or stream and there baptize scores of converts while the town turned out to witness the spectacle. At times several ministers took part in baptizing the long lines of converts.

One traveling evangelist sometimes performed midnight baptisms. After preaching until midnight, he led the congregation to the river and there baptized those who made professions of faith during the service.

These midnight processionals often led through the streets of the city. During the procession the congregation would sing hymns and cry out to aroused sleepers, "Come to Christ! Come to Christ!"

One evangelist visiting a seaport town had a woman convert who wanted to be baptized immediately. Converts were usually baptized in the harbor, and since a storm had come up, the evangelist thought the baptism should be delayed.

The woman persisted, however, and led the way through a driving rain and high winds to the ocean. During the baptism she and the preacher were swept under by high waves, but they were rescued, and the woman went away rejoicing.

Baptism under cover of darkness.

PREACHER Paid Husband After Baptizing Wife

Baptist insistence upon believer's baptism by immersion has provoked unusual responses at times.

The state-supported church has persecuted Baptists for their beliefs, mobs have attempted to break up baptisms, one group dipped dogs in ridiculing Baptist baptism, and an irate husband shot a preacher for baptizing his wife.

One of the most unusual responses was that of a husband in Missouri more than 100 years ago. When the husband heard that his wife had been baptized, he threatened to leave her unless she left the Baptist church.

Hoping to reconcile the enraged husband, the preacher who had performed the baptism visited him. After a long discussion, the husband made the preacher a proposition: "If you will pay me $15, I will say no more about the matter and will be satisfied."

The preacher's response was as unusual as the husband's. He accepted the offer, paid the husband $15, and the matter was settled.

ARE Non-Baptists Christians? Asked Landmark Movement

Should Baptists recognize members of other churches as true Christians? This was a question many Baptists struggled with as "Landmarkism" arose not long after the Southern Baptist Convention was formed.

Landmarkism began as a movement to restore the "purity" of the New Testament church. Landmarkers not only called into question the Christian experience of other believers, but questioned whether any but Baptists were true ministers of the gospel or whether non-Baptist churches were true churches.

Because Landmarkers believed that only Baptist churches were true to the New Testament, members of other churches were not true Christians. By the same token, ministers of these churches were not true ministers of the gospel. And because other churches did not practice believer's baptism, they were not true churches. These were some of the "old landmarks" that Landmarkers believed should be reset.

Landmarkers also opposed pulpit exchange, alien immersion, open communion, and other practices. Because they believed in the absolute primacy of the local church, they also opposed boards, agencies, and conventions.

The Landmark controversy continued into the twentieth

century. Traces of it may still be found among Baptist churches today.

❧

DRUNKEN Father Interrupted Baptism of His Daughter

Not everyone welcomed the evangelistic efforts of zealous nineteenth-century Baptist preachers.

As one Baptist evangelist led a group of converts into a New York river for baptism, the drunken father of a young girl dashed into the water to prevent her baptism. The evangelist tried to reassure the father that his daughter would not be baptized against his wishes, but the father seized his daughter and struggled drunkenly with the preacher. Although a peace officer stood watching the baptism, he made no effort to prevent the disruption of a religious service.

Later the father came to the evangelist, charging that he had been injured in the struggle and demanding settlement. When the preacher refused, the father swore out a warrant for his arrest. The county court later dismissed the case.

❧

TWO Giants Playing "Last Tag" Produced Sunday School Board

Two giants of the denomination played "last tag" in a hotel room at Birmingham, Alabama, to produce the Baptist Sunday School Board (1891).

For almost thirty years, Sunday school literature had been produced by the Home Mission Board. But the printing and distribution of these materials had become too big a task for that board to handle as a sideline.

In 1890 James M. Frost, a Richmond, Virginia, pastor who was to become the first secretary of the Sunday School Board, introduced a Convention resolution calling for the formation of a publication board. Frost was opposed by J. B. Gambrell

Frost and Gambrell discuss the formation of the Sunday School Board.

of Mississippi, who wanted the Home Mission Board to continue publication.

The Convention placed the matter in the hands of a Sunday School Committee which was to report the following year in Birmingham. This committee appointed Frost and Gambrell to draw up a report.

The two opposing leaders grappled with their differences most of the day in a Birmingham hotel. Finally, Gambrell made Frost an offer he could not refuse. He suggested that Frost write the report and even name the location of the proposed Sunday School Board. But the offer had a catch: Gambrell wanted to write the last paragraph of the report.

Frost agreed, but with one further stipulation: Frost would append one final sentence to Gambrell's last paragraph.

Gambrell wrote: "In conclusion your committee, in its long and earnest consideration of this whole matter in all its environments, has been compelled to take account of the well-known fact, that there are widely divergent views held among us by brethren equally earnest, consecrated and devoted to the best interest of the Master's Kingdom. It is therefore recommended that the fullest freedom of choice be accorded to everyone as to what literature he will use or support, and that no brother be disparaged in the slightest degree on account of what he may do in the exercise of his right as Christ's freeman."

To which Frost added: "But we would earnestly urge all brethren to give to this Board a fair consideration, and in no case to obstruct it in the great work assigned by this Convention."

When the time came for the report of the Sunday School Committee, the Convention hall was so packed that Frost had to be lifted through a window and helped to the rostrum. The report was adopted with few dissenting votes. One historian wrote: "It is doubtful if the Southern Baptist Convention has ever witnessed a more sublime moment."

FOOTWASHING Ceremony Solved Sticky Problem for Students

Cries of "Fire!" awakened ministerial students in New York Hall of Southern Baptist Theological Seminary, Louisville, Kentucky, on a chill night in October, 1892.

As the barefooted, pajama-clad students reached the hall of their dormitory, they were riveted to the floor. Fear had not gripped them, however. Their feet were held fast by molasses. Pranksters had poured molasses in the hall and then routed the sleeping students with their false alarm.

John A. Broadus

The faculty was outraged by the prank. On the motion of Dr. A. T. Robertson, it was resolved that seminary president John A. Broadus should address the students, "setting forth the mortification felt by the faculty on account of the uproar."

The mortification of the faculty no doubt would have been even greater if they, like the students, had been forced to engage in a midnight "footwashing ceremony" to remove the sticky molasses.

Seminary students of that day did not spend all their time in pranks, however. Final examinations began at eight o'clock in the morning and lasted until six in the afternoon. Lunch was brought in to the students, who were not allowed to discuss the examination during this break. Students sometimes broke under the strain of these long and demanding examinations.

SOUTH'S Oldest Baptist Church Has Survived Many Hardships

The oldest Baptist church in the South, the First Baptist Church of Charleston, South Carolina, has survived war, flood, earthquake, cyclone, and other obstacles.

The old church building was damaged by flood waters and winds in 1752, and church records were destroyed.

When the British seized Charleston in 1780, the church property was confiscated and the building used as a storehouse —perhaps in retaliation for staunch Baptist support of the fight for American independence.

During the Civil War the church was damaged again when shells exploded in the building, shattering the organ and causing other damage.

A cyclone unroofed the building in 1885, and rain poured in, causing heavy damage to the interior.

The church had scarcely recovered from this blow when an earthquake shook the building in 1886, damaging the building and furnishings.

The church traces its beginnings to 1682 when William Screven led in organizing a Baptist church in Maine. Driven by persecution, Screven led a part of the congregation South and settled in the South Carolina wilderness near the present site of Charleston.

In 1699 the lot on which the present building stands was given to the church. The church was organized 100 years before Charleston was incorporated.

Richard Furman, who became pastor in 1787, was one of the church's many outstanding leaders. He was elected the first president of the Triennial Convention when that national Baptist body was formed in 1814. Furman also served as a delegate to the South Carolina Constitutional Convention. He led in the formation of the South Carolina Baptist Convention, first in the South, and was its first president. The church also led in the formation of Furman University, first Baptist university in the South.

Another outstanding pastor was Oliver Hart, called in 1749. Hart led in the formation of the Charleston Association, first in the South. In 1755 the association sent out John Gano, first associational missionary in the South.

Two founders of Southern Baptist Theological Seminary, James P. Boyce, first seminary president, and Basil Manly, Jr., were members of the church. It was widely influential in education, theology, missions, and church organization.

Before the Civil War the church included some 300 slaves. They often filled the balcony to overflowing and added much to the services with their fervor and spirited singing.

FARMER Lost His Oats But His Soul Was Saved

Before the days of the automobile and motels, visiting evangelists usually stayed in the home of the host pastor or with one of the church members. Pastors carefully selected these hosts. Usually the evangelist was lodged with a wealthy member, where he would be comfortable and well fed, or with a more devout member, where he could enjoy discussing religion.

At other times, however, the evangelist was lodged with an unbeliever in the hope that this close association might lead the sinner to repentance and faith.

During a revival in Virginia, an evangelist was the guest of an unbelieving farmer. As soon as the preacher arrived, the farmer launched an attack on preachers, churches, and revivals.

On the day the revival began, the farmer announced that his oats were rotting in the field, and he could not attend church. When the preacher insisted, the farmer replied, "There is no use talking. I have been out to look at the oats, and they are in very bad condition. I cannot think about going to church today."

"Let the oats rot," said the preacher. "Your soul is worth

more than all the oats in the world."

The farmer finally yielded and at church made a profession of faith. Some time later the evangelist saw him and asked about the crop of oats.

"Every grain rotted," the farmer said with a smile.

"I'm glad they did," said the preacher. "If they hadn't, you might have supposed that the Lord worked a miracle to reward you for going to church, and the Lord does not bribe people to be converted."

WOMAN'S Faith Helped Establish First Baptist Church in Texas

Texas of 150 years ago was no place for the faint hearted as early settlers fought with Indians and Mexicans. Yet, none of those pioneers was more courageous than a Baptist woman, Massy Sparks Millard.

"Aunt Massy," as she was called, settled with her husband and children near Nacogdoches, Texas. During the day she often poured bullets for the men's rifles and at night sought protection in a grove near the house while the men fought night raiders.

In the darkness of the grove, "Aunt Massy" gathered her children to pray for God's protection and for the safety of the men. Other women and children of the community also sought refuge in the grove and joined her prayer meetings.

The little band found more than safety in the grove. They also found they could worship undetected by the authorities, who favored Catholic worship only. The women prayed for their families, and for a better day for Texas. They prayed for freedom to worship as Baptists. God soon answered their prayers.

Isaac Reed, a Baptist preacher from Tennessee, settled near Nacogdoches. He preached from house to house in spite of much opposition and held outdoor meetings not far from where "Aunt

Massy" and her friends held their prayer meetings. He led settlers to build a combination meetinghouse and schoolhouse of oak logs. A church was gathered, called Union Church, because it included members of various denominations.

In 1838, Reed and Robert G. Green organized a Baptist church, composed of nine members, including two slaves. Reed is believed to be the first Baptist to administer baptism in Texas.

Today Reed's church, Old North, is the oldest Baptist church in Texas. In the church yard is a large oak, believed to be the tree which once sheltered "Aunt Massy" Millard and her prayer meeting band.

MONEY Where the Need Was

Before the formation of the Southern Baptist Convention, Jesse Mercer, a leading Georgia Baptist, deposited $2,500 with the Home Mission Society of New York to send home missionaries to Texas.

His friends warned "Father Mercer" that he was throwing his money away. Texas, he was informed, was then infested with thieves, murderers, and scoundrels, a haven for fugitives and outlaws.

"You had better not tell me any more about such characters in Texas," Mercer responded, "or I'll be compelled to double the amount and set aside $5,000."

PERSECUTION, Hardships Overcome By First Baptists in Mississippi

Persecution or attack by the British, Tories, Indians, Spaniards, and Catholics could not discourage the hardy pioneers who established the Woodville Baptist Church, oldest Baptist church in Mississippi.

During the Revolutionary War, Richard Curtis, Sr., a Baptist deacon, fought against the British in South Carolina with

Francis Marion, the "old swamp fox." Because of their activities with Marion, Curtis and others were hunted by the British and their homes plundered by Tories.

To escape persecution, Curtis, his family, and others moved westward. As they traveled down the Tennessee River, they were attacked by Indians, and many were slaughtered. They finally settled on Cole's Creek near Natchez. The settlers met for worship, called Richard Curtis, Jr., to preach, and in 1791 formed the Cole's Creek or Salem Baptist Church.

Spanish Catholics were in control of Mississippi and soon forced Curtis and some of his followers to return to South Carolina. When Curtis came back to Mississippi after the Spanish lost control, he assisted in forming an arm of the Cole's Creek Church called "The Baptist Church on Buffaloe."

This church was to become the Woodville Baptist Church. The Mississippi legislature granted a charter to "The Baptist Meeting House in Woodville" in 1824.

The old auditorium was constructed in 1809 by slave labor, using brick made on the grounds. Black people were active in the church for many years and even outnumbered the whites until the eve of the Civil War.

NO ONE Far from Preacher In Twelve Corners Church

Although it is unusual, the Twelve Corners Baptist Church of Garfield, Arkansas, is not unique. It was patterned after a similar church in Tennessee.

The church was organized in 1842 as the Sugar Creek Baptist Church. Services were suspended during the Civil War, when marauders destroyed the church records.

Nineteen members met and reorganized the church in 1865, naming it Twelve Corners after a church in Lascassas, Tennessee. Many early members of the Arkansas church were from Tennessee or were descendants of Tennessee families.

The log meetinghouse was constructed of four sections, forming twelve corners. Thus, it was possible to construct of logs a large auditorium in which the entire congregation could see the preacher.

The logs used in construction of the original building were hand dressed in local mills. Benches, tables, and other furniture also were hand-made.

The first building was destroyed by fire. The present building, a replica of the first, was built in 1896.

DANCING into Darkness?

Before the beginning of this century, churches were open in their condemnation of such "worldly pleasures" as dancing, the theater, horse racing, card playing, gambling, baseball, and football.

The following diatribe against dancing appeared in one of the state Baptist papers of that day.

> *"I never knew a decidedly pious Christian—I mean one that lives in the enjoyment of religion—who at any time advocated or practiced the sinful amusement of dancing. I have seen many who, in their sinful days, passionately loved the sin of dancing, but after their conversion could not look upon it with the least degree of allowance. To my mind the strongest evidence of the sinfulness of dancing—outside of the Bible, which condemns 'all ungodliness and worldly lusts,' together with all kinds of* revelings*—is, that it is so popular with the fashionable world and formal backslidden Christians, and that it is one of the chief means by which the enemy of souls succeeds, in so many instances, in enticing young and unwary Christians from the strait and narrow way that leads to heaven.*

FATHER, Son, Grandson Served Oldest Georgia Church

The oldest Baptist church in Georgia, the Kiokee Baptist Church near Augusta, was served by father, son, and grandson as pastors during the first sixty years of the church's life.

Daniel Marshall was pastor of the church during the Revolutionary War and afterward. He was once arrested by Tories but preached to both British and American troops during the war. He was the first moderator of the Georgia Association, first in the state. From this association grew the Georgia Baptist Convention.

Daniel was succeeded by his son, Abraham, and his grandson, Jabez. Abraham led in the organization of about forty churches.

Discipline was strict during the early days of the church. Members might be dismissed for swearing, failure to govern their families well, or failure to attend worship or business meetings. In 1894, a resolution was introduced condemning "the practice of baseball and attending the playing of baseball."

First mention in church records of women holding places of responsibility was in 1869, when several were appointed to a committee to receive contributions for the support of missions.

Early church caretakers were always paid, while pastors never were. For this reason, pastors often served as caretakers in order to be assured of the income—$10 a year.

Before the Civil War, black members outnumbered whites at Kiokee by six to one.

PASTOR, Deacons Followed Outlaw into Texas

Before Texas was admitted to the union, the territory was a haven for outlaws and scoundrels. When a fugitive from justice crossed the Sabine River, separating the Texas territory from Louisiana, he was safe from the law.

One day a ferryman, operating a ferry across the Sabine, noticed a man waving frantically to him from the Louisiana side of the river. He crossed quickly and transported his passenger to the Texas territory. Just as they touched on the Texas side, a posse arrived on the Louisiana side.

The fugitive waved at his pursuers and shouted: "I'm too fast for you. You have no authority outside the United States. I'm safe here."

Then the fugitive kissed the ground where he stood and shouted: "The Sabine River is a greater savior than Jesus Christ! He only saves men from hell when they die; but this river saves living men from prison."

Some time later the ferryman was taking a load of passengers across the river. The party included a Baptist preacher, two deacons, a doctor, and a lawyer. He told the party about the escape of the fleeing fugitive and then asked, "And, gentlemen, what have you done that you should have come to Texas?"

The men looked at one another, but none of them had an answer for the ferryman.

AFTER Unimpressive Start, Raleigh Church Progressed

From an unimpressive beginning, the First Baptist Church of Raleigh, North Carolina, became one of the leading churches of the Southern Baptist Convention.

The church was formed in 1812 by twenty-three members dismissed from another church. Fourteen of these were Negro slaves. The church met in homes or public halls until a building was erected.

In 1835, there was a church split. The minority group lost the church property and again worshiped in public places and in the homes of members.

When a new church building was dedicated in 1858, the congregation totaled 228 white and 207 black members. Slaves continued to worship in the Raleigh church through the stormy days of the Civil War. In 1868, about 200 black members of the church were granted letters and formed a separate church in Raleigh.

Shortly after the close of the Civil War, the pastor and an

evangelist conducted a seven-week revival. More than 200 professions of faith were recorded, including a number of Union soldiers quartered in Raleigh at the time.

PIONEER Preacher Had to Prove Himself

Preachers on the frontier had to "first prove themselves"—and for good reason.

A man posing as a Baptist preacher entered a settlement in the Old West and claimed that he was destitute. Filled with compassion, residents promptly made a collection for the stranger in their midst. Later the imposter was seen squandering the offering at a local race track.

Incidents such as this led preachers in some communities to form "vigilance committees." One committee published in the local newspaper the names of all licensed preachers in the area and required any visiting preacher to present "unmistakable credentials" from his denomination.

The vigilance committee urged churches to regard as a "suspicious character" any visiting preacher who took offense because his papers were demanded before he occupied the pulpit.

COFFEE Kept Her from Church, Said Woman in Testimonial

Coffee drinking can bring on many ills, including preventing one from attending church, Baptists of an earlier day were warned.

The following testimonial appeared in the news columns of a state Baptist paper in 1901.

> *"When a person has to keep the feet out from under the cover during the coldest nights in winter because of the heat and prickly sensation, it is time that coffee, which causes the trouble, be left off.*

"There is no end to the nervous conditions that coffee will produce. It shows in one way in one person and in another way in another. In this case, the lady lived in Vermillion, South Dakota.

"She says: 'I have to lie awake half the night with my feet and limbs out of the bed on the coldest nights and feel afraid to sleep for fear of catching cold. I had been troubled for years with twitching and jerking of the lower limbs, and for most of the time I have been unable to go to church or lectures because of that awful feeling that I must keep on the move.

" 'When it was brought to my attention that coffee caused many nervous diseases, I concluded to drop coffee and take P—— Food Coffee to see if my trouble was caused by coffee drinking. I only drank one cup of coffee for breakfast, but that was enough for me. When I quit it my troubles disappeared in an almost miraculous way. Now I have no more of the twitching and jerking and can sleep with any amount of bedding over me and sleep all night, in sound, peaceful rest.

" 'P—— Food Coffee is absolutely worth its weight in gold to me.' "

BLOW from Walking Stick Restored Order at Revival

Lack of a suitable meetinghouse sometimes presented unusual problems for congregations in pioneer areas.

A revival meeting was scheduled in a billiard hall on Main Street of a town in the Old West. As worshipers gathered inside the billiard hall, drunks and rowdies gathered outside the hall. The unbelievers were determined to break up the meeting.

As the congregation inside the hall began to sing, a drunk on the outside pulled on the neck of a hen he held under his arm. The hen squawked in protest above the sound of the singers.

To further disrupt the meeting, one of the rowdies stuck his head in the window of the hall and shouted at the top of his lungs, "Glory to God!" Those on the outside chorused in response, "Amen! Amen!"

A Baptist preacher posted himself near the window. As the ruffian stuck his head inside to shout, the preacher clouted him on the head with his walking stick. Then he warned those on the outside that some of the worshipers had brought their firearms as protection against the Indians and that further interruptions would be met with a more violent protest.

The worship service was concluded, but as the worshipers departed, they saw several drunks waiting outside. Apparently they intended to give the Baptist preacher a beating for hitting one of their number with his walking stick.

As the preacher left the hall, he was accompanied by a colonel who had won fame as a fighter against the Mexicans and Indians. "If there is to be any fighting," the colonel said to the ruffians, "I want it known that I am on the side of law and order and religious liberty."

He and the preacher then left the billiard hall without further interference.

A "TIN-HEADED Linsey-Woolsey"?

Pioneer Baptists may have been lacking in formal education, but they were a plainspoken people who knew how to communicate. Terms such as "linsey-woolsey," tin-headed," and "iron-jacket" conveyed definite meanings to Baptists of that day.

A "linsey-woolsey" was one who believed that works as well as grace were necessary for salvation. The term came from the fact that Old Testament priests were not allowed to wear garments made of wool and linen. They were required to wear either all wool or all linen.

One who sacrificed principles for popularity was "tin-headed." Tin, a soft metal, is easily dented by a hammer. The preacher or church leader whose head was soft enough to be turned by popularity earned this name.

An "iron-jacket" was one with antimissionary convictions. These regarded with suspicion any organized effort that seemed to pose a threat to the autonomy of the local church.

❧

CIGARETTE Is Boys' Worst Enemy, Writer Warned in State Paper

Cigarette packages of a half century ago carried no warning by the Surgeon General, but Baptists of that day could not say they were not warned of the evil effects of smoking.

A writer in one of the state Baptist papers declared that cigarette smoking not only was injurious to the health but also led to countless other problems. A part of the warning follows.

> *"The worst enemy of our boys today is the cigarette.*
>
> *"A narcotic of any kind will destroy the will power and enfeeble the brain. Cigarette smoking will make the boy or girl a coward, will interfere with their studies, and will make them dishonest, impure, and criminal.*
>
> *"The cigarette will deprive a boy of a good position and keep him from getting another. It introduces him into vicious and indolent society. The time will come when the cigarette will not suffice and then the participant will resort to whiskey, morphine, etc.*
>
> *"Young lady, do not permit your young man friends to smoke a cigarette in your presence. Be firm and plain with them. You will help them and humanity.*
>
> *"Young ladies who attend the boarding schools in our fair Southland, never compromise yourselves and smoke a cigarette with your classmates; if you do, you will regret it some day. It is a fact that cigarettes are smoked by some girls in all boarding schools, we are sorry to say."*

❧

TENTS for the Wilderness

Some Baptists on the frontier believed quite literally in "tenting in the wilderness." The following resolution appears in the minutes of one association.

> "RESOLVED, *That this association recommend to the prayerful consideration of all the friends of the Redeemer, that, in*

place of building tents out of wood on such occasions, each head of a family make a tent of cloth, and take their wagon, with forage enough to feed their horses for a few days, and enough of light diet to feed their families, and approach the door of the sanctuary, as the Israelites did the tabernacle, and take God at his word, and lay hold of his promises, and see if he will not pour you out a blessing that will fill your heart with gladness, and make you rejoice in place of mourn when you come to press a dying pillow."

PREACHER Spun Yarn To Snare "Outsiders"

During the days of the log cabin church on the frontier—as today—not everyone went to church to worship.

The church was a gathering place, a place to see friends and to socialize. Some of the men who went to church with their families remained outside the meetinghouse on the church grounds. There they laughed and joked and swapped yarns, much to the annoyance of the preacher and congregation inside the church.

One Baptist preacher in Texas decided that he must beat these story tellers at their own game. After trying unsuccessfully to get the men inside the church for worship, he challenged them.

"If I cannot spin a better yarn than you," the preacher said, "then I will quit preaching and listen to you." The men accepted the challenge and gave him rapt attention.

The preacher then recalled a story of the fighting between the Texans led by Sam Houston and the Mexicans led by Santa Ana. A band of disloyal Texans who thought surely that Santa Ana and his superior forces would be victorious sent the Mexican general their pledge that after he won the battle they would be his loyal subjects.

As the cannons of Santa Ana roared and thundered, the turncoats shouted, "Hurrah for Santa Ana!" Then the Mexicans ran low on ammunition, and the roar of the cannons subsided.

But the crackle of Texas rifles could still be heard.

When it became apparent that the Texans would win the battle, the turncoats again changed their tune. They began to shout, "Hurrah for Sam Houston!"

"I would not be surprised," the preacher concluded, "if that same band is not today a bunch of backslidden Baptists who go to church regularly but stand around on the outside and tell stories during the sermon. Such men always want to be on the popular side. When it is popular to dance, drink, and tell stories, they are on that side. But when religion is popular, they are on that side."

As the congregation beamed approval, the preacher asked, "Now, gentlemen, will you proceed or shall I?"

The men were subdued. "You have the floor, preacher," a spokesman said. "We give it up." After that the men became a part of the worshiping congregation.

THEATER a Menace, Editorial Writer Warned

One of the major threats to the church around the turn of this century was the theater, according to many leading Baptists.

"The extent to which the church can tolerate theatergoing is one of the greatest and most perplexing problems of today," said an editorial writer in one of the state Baptist papers. But as he wrote further, it became clear that he did not believe the church should tolerate much, if any, theatergoing by its members.

"I have never seen a soul-winning, theatergoing church member," he wrote. "It perverts the intellect by sensationalism and spectacular displays. No church man will cling to his Bible whose mind is trained in such a school. It begets extravagance and is a waste of money. I know plenty of church members who pay more for theater tickets in one month than they give to the church in an entire year.

"The play is said to be a warning of the bad results of sin, but, strange to say, its promoters use in their advertising bills the scenes most calculated to attract a crowd which desires the low and vulgar. The play was witnessed by men and women together, when to have talked together about the plot in private would have been considered vulgar in the extreme.

"It begets idleness and incapacity for business. Many businessmen have told me that they can see in the results of sales when their clerks are full of the theater. Certainly indifference to church work will result. I do not know a single theater-lover who is a good prayer meetingite.

"The purpose of the theater is to degrade. As an institution it is keyed to lust. The sickening love scenes and silly flirtations that must be injected into almost every play are but pandering to this object."

WILD Ride on Mustang Left Preacher Bruised

Preachers of today, who drive hundreds of miles in a day over broad interstate highways, or hop from coast to coast in jet liners, can scarcely appreciate the problems encountered by traveling preachers of horse-and-buggy days.

Highways were unknown in that day. Itinerant preachers on the frontier found their way from settlement to settlement by means of Indian and animal trails. When they came to a river, usually the only means of crossing was by swimming. Inns or taverns were scarce and often crowded and filthy. Frequently the only available accommodation was the hospitality of a stranger and his log cabin.

As one Baptist preacher traveled in the Old West, his horse became lame. The preacher was forced to exchange his mount for a mustang that was scarcely broken to harness. To insure a safer ride, the preacher fastened a forked stick to the horse's girth and the fork end of the stick to the cheeks of the bridle. Thus, the horse was unable to lower its head and buck the rider off.

The preacher continued his travels without incident, but he tired of the stares and questions of the curious regarding the unusual harness he had put on the mustang. At last, horse and rider came to a wide river. After the horse had swum across, it was near exhaustion. The preacher decided that the mustang was too tired to buck, and he removed the forked stick.

He had not been in the saddle long, however, before the horse lowered its head and began to buck and pitch. The preacher's hat flew in one direction, his umbrella in another, and his saddlebags and blanket in still another. As the horse reared and tossed, the preacher looked about for a soft spot of ground on which to land.

The preacher finally reached his appointment, but he was so bruised and sore from his wild ride that he was forced to preach without his accustomed vigor and animation.

PREACHER Believed His Ministry More Important than Machinery

In order to provide for their families, many pioneer preachers had to be hunters, trappers, cobblers, carpenters, and farmers. They usually received little or nothing for their services as pastors.

Z. N. Morrell, a Baptist preacher and one of the early settlers of Texas, was an excellent farmer. He developed a number of labor-saving devices to aid farmers. One was a planter which plowed a furrow, dropped in the corn, and covered the seed, all in one operation.

As Morrell demonstrated the planter to skeptical neighbors, one of them asked the man who was operating the machine if it worked. He replied that it "planted corn with so little labor on my part that I am afraid it is of no account."

Morrell's friends urged him to secure a patent on his planter, but he declined. He feared that work on the machine might take too much time from his ministry and divert his mind from study of the Word.

EDITOR'S Son Had Last Word In Writing of "Football Mania"

The then-current "football mania" drew the ire of a state Baptist paper editor around the turn of this century. Deploring the "brutal" sport, he wrote as follows:

> *"We may say, because of our sympathy for them who engage in the game of football, that we sincerely regret that this game has been imported from England to our own America. We are aware that we will encounter the students at Mercer and the State University, who lately engaged in a most exciting game. But their opposition must not deter us from speaking out now as this mania is seizing many of sporting disposition in this country.*
>
> *"If modern football were the same as that in which our fathers found wholesome recreation, we should remain silent. The same as now played simply brings out the physical athletic skill of the boys or men on either side. The earnestness, and we may say desperateness, reminds one of the gladiatorial contests in the days of ancient Rome.*
>
> *"In England, and we may say too in this country, it appears that leading institutions of learning set more upon a victory by their students than upon intellectual scholarship. The contest between Yale and Princeton recently is said to have drawn twenty times more people of the educated class than a match in which mental culture between twenty young men put on trial would draw.*
>
> *"Some of the scenes in these football contests are said to be brutal, and the players are seriously injured and have to leave the field. In many cases in England fatal results have come to some of the players."*

A few issues later there was a letter to the editor on the subject of football. It was from the editor's twelve-year-old son:

"I read in your paper about football. I would like to express my opinion of the game. Develop the muscles and boldness of your sons by giving them a football. By developing the boldness of the boys, I mean, give them courage to go up into the crowd if they do get kicked on the shins. Suppose our country should have a war when 'we' boys become men, and are fighting for our country we will need the boldness and courage that our football gave us."

The effect of this letter on the editor's viewpoint was amazing. He replied, "The father showed himself a worthy sire of this promising son since he bears in his body the honorable scars of bravely-fought battles."

After confessing that he had been out kicking a football with his son, the editor filed this scouting report: "The editor advises one of the college teams to engage him, at once."

Apparently the editor saw no contradiction between deploring the brutality of football while praising the "honorable scars" of war.

BAPTISTS Proud of Sam Houston

Texas Baptists are prouder of no convert than the beloved Sam Houston, "hero of San Jacinto" and leader of the fight for Texas freedom from Mexico.

A former governor of Tennessee, Houston led his Texas army to victory over the Mexican forces of Santa Ana. He was

Sam Houston

elected the first president of the Texas Republic. After Texas was admitted to the union, he served as governor.

Houston was baptized on November 19, 1854, in the Baptist church at Independence, Texas. He was active in church affairs and addressed the state Baptist convention.

The Texas statesman died in 1863. A few days before his death, Houston was visited by Z. N. Morrell, a Baptist preacher. Morrell recorded that Houston faced death calmly, confident in his faith in Christ.

AS IN All Barbarous Nations, The Women Slit Their Ears

Women's fashions apparently were as bewildering 100 years ago as they are today. A state Baptist paper of that day quoted as follows a letter from a member of the Japanese Embassy stationed in Washington.

> *"We find it very difficult to comply with the demands of our sovereign, forbidding us to touch the women of this country. Not from any disposition on our part to disobey, but from their desire to seize us by the hand.*
>
> *"They are apparently allowed here the greatest freedom, but it is only in appearance. Every woman, married or single, is fastened in a cage of bamboo or flexible steel, extending from the waist to the feet. This seems to be so arranged to give them no uneasiness, but they are much ashamed of it, and conceal it under so many coverings that it renders their appearance ludicrous.*
>
> *"They are unrestricted as to the appearance of the upper part of their persons, which they are permitted to display as much as they wish. This they seem to avail themselves of, and on all occasions of high ceremony wear very low dresses.*
>
> *"As in all barbarous nations, they slit their ears and suspend from them ornaments of gold and silver. They also paint and powder themselves, and after greasing their hair, twist it into fantastic shapes and fasten it with long pins and combs.*
>
> *"Some of them would be fine looking, if they did not disfigure themselves by the hideous and vulgar custom of eyebrows and keeping their teeth white.*

"Be assured, therefore, we are in no danger of being captivated by their appearance; we feel nothing but regret that the barbarous and absurd customs of men should thus destroy the charms which cultivation and refinement would so much improve."

An editorial note accompanying the letter did not agree that the letter writer was in no danger of being captivated. The note observed that the letter writer "has been rather a close observer of the fair sex" and commented that if the Japanese were a married man "his better half should secure his immediate recall."

PICTURE Show Called "Breeder of Evil"

There was no television or crime in the streets fifty years ago to blame for poor Sunday night church attendance. But the church of that day also had its competition. While some viewers today are wondering if they have seen the last of the picture show, a half century ago it was regarded as a major threat to both church and state.

A state Baptist paper of that day devoted a full front page to an editorial warning of the evils of the picture show. Part of the editorial follows:

"It seems that the moving picture shows are here to stay, and instead of decreasing they are multiplying. After a close study of the few we saw, we are of the opinion that the moving picture shows are breeders of evil.

"Perhaps the least evil of the picture shows is the large amount of money being spent on them that might be used to better advantage. Thousands and thousands of people without homes of their own and with scant supplies of food and raiment spend a part of their meager earning to see the ever changing reels that come and go. If these nickels and dimes were put into a savings bank, they would become a nest egg of material independence which would mean a substantial citizenship.

"In most cities the picture show is in competition with the churches, as they are in full blast on Sunday, which is the big day. On Sunday evening while in a large city we attended services

at the largest and most influential Baptist church. It was a beautiful evening, and we feared we would have difficulty in securing a seat, even in the galleries. But to our dismay, the auditorium numbered less than 130, and they were mostly women of middle age and past. On our return to the hotel we passed several picture shows, and there were swarms of young people going in and coming out. It does not take a prophet to foretell the future of the churches where such conditions maintain.

"A more serious thing still is the part the female plays in films. In nearly every instance there is a brief courtship, followed by an engagement, sealed with a kiss, including an embrace. The fruitage of such pictures is an undue familiarity between the sexes, and that on short acquaintance.

"It seems to us it is time to call a halt.

"Many mothers and fathers would lift up their hands in holy horror if they knew their sons and daughters were reading such books as Jesse James, and yet they furnish the money and give their consent for them to see things portrayed in the picture shows many fold worse than those portrayed in the story of Jesse James.

"How much the picture show is chargeable for the present tidal wave of vice and crime, we cannot tell; but it is certain that the picture shows as we now have them are a menace to both the church and State."

WEDDING Began at a Gallop, Ended in a Slow Trot

Firing revolvers into the air, cracking seventeen-foot cow whips, and whooping and yelling at the top of their lungs, the party of about fifty horsemen raced across the fields toward a house in the clearing.

It was not a cavalry charge; it was a wedding party. The bridegroom was at the head of the party, his groomsmen at his side. Close behind them were other friends of the groom. They were "running up" the groom to the home of his bride, where the wedding was to take place. It was a cherished custom among pioneer families of one hundred years ago.

At the bride's house the groom and his party reined up in a cloud of dust and leaped from their mounts. Inside, the bride waited with her maids and family. The Baptist preacher was on hand to perform the ceremony.

The bride, dressed in white with ribbons at her neck and waist and a garland of evergreens in her hair, came with her maids to the porch or piazza of the log house. There she met the groom and his men, and together they faced the preacher. He pronounced the words that joined them for life, for divorce was a rarity in those days.

From miles around, neighbors and friends had gathered for the wedding party. They came in wagons, in buggies, in ox carts, on horseback, and on foot. The size of the party depended on the prominence and popularity of the bride and groom.

The bride, her mother, and friends had been busy for weeks. The house was appropriately decorated, but the main attraction was the dinner. Eating began soon after the ceremony was performed. Tables were piled high with stacks of potato custards, mountains of ginger cakes and cookies, and huge platters of chicken pot pies, baked chicken and turkey, boiled ham, roast beef, sliced venison, sausage, souse, pork, pickles, relishes, pound cakes, layer cakes, cinnamon cakes, angel cakes —all homemade, of course. In the center of the bounty was the bride's cake, layers pyramided one on top of the other with a frosted and garnished apple at the summit.

In those days hard-working men prided themselves on enormous appetites, and their womenfolk in turn prided themselves on their ability to outcook even those ravenous appetites. The feast usually began about noon and continued until sunset warned the guests that it was time to begin the return trip home before dark.

The groom's party that came riding up at a full gallop left at a more leisurely pace, their belts let out to the last notch.

☙

DEATH Was Near, Real In Homes of Pioneers

Because there were no hospitals or morticians or funeral homes, and few doctors, on the frontier, death was near and real to pioneer families of another century.

Friends and neighbors came to "set up" all night for weeks when there was a critical illness in a home. Perhaps this was done because, in that day of primitive medicine, no one knew anything else to do in the face of terminal illness.

When death at last came, there was no time to waste. The corpse, dressed in the best that the deceased had, was laid out on a "cooling board." There coins were placed on the eyelids, a handkerchief was tied around the jaws, the hands were folded on the breast, the feet were bound, and a sheet covered the remains.

The coffinmakers came next. They measured the corpse with a rule, then took a wagon to the saw mill for seasoned pine planks which were kept for this purpose. Another went to the community store for nails, screws, and black and white cloth.

The bottom, lid, and ends of the coffin were easily made, but the sides called for more skill. One-third the length down, the side boards were sawed half way through with cuts about a quarter-inch apart. The wood between the cuts was chiseled out. Next, streaming water was poured on the boards at the cuts, and the wood was bent without breaking to the familiar coffin shape. The outside of the coffin was covered with black cloth. The inside was first lined with cotton batting and covered with white cloth.

Meanwhile, a preacher was summoned, often the same one who had baptized and married the deceased. The little procession made its way to the cemetery where men had been digging the grave, while others made the coffin. The traditional grave for an adult was three feet by seven feet by three feet deep. Graves were not as deep when they were dug by hand.

The graveside funeral was simple and brief. Usually a

hymn was sung.

"No chilling winds nor pois'nous breath
Can reach that healthful shore;
Sickness and sorrow, pain and death,
Are felt and feared no more."

Then those who dug the grave covered it over with their shovels and hoes, and a mound was carefully fashioned to represent the bulk of the coffin beneath. After boards were set at the head and foot, the procession returned home.

It was a simple and crude means of burial, but it was used to lay to rest some of the greatest men this country has ever produced.

CHURCH Organ Was Seen But Not Heard in Worship

A Baptist church in Tennessee permitted an organ to be brought into the church—provided it was never played during worship services.

Today, when church staffs include ministers of music who direct graded choir programs, and when Sunday Schools are "the evangelistic arms of the church," it is hard to believe that once these organizations were "taboo" in many Baptist churches.

The "anti" spirit which pervaded many churches more than a hundred years ago frowned on missionary organizations, Sunday Schools, music programs and musical instruments, Bible societies, agencies and conventions—almost anything, in fact, that was not directly controlled by the local church.

The Tennessee church permitted an organ to be placed in the church, but ruled that it was not to be played during worship services. The organ could be played, however, during the Sunday School period. The Sunday School was still a "stepchild" of the church, and since members regarded the school as questionable at best they decided that the playing of the organ at that time was no more offensive than the Sunday School itself.

Not until the organ was in the church many years and most members had forgotten the old ruling was it ever played during worship services.

DINNER, Singing Were Highlights Of Annual Sunday School Celebration

Sunday Schools have not always been the integral part of church life that they are today. The Sunday School movement began outside the church, was at first given only grudging admittance, and only after many years of struggle did it become the "outreach arm" of today's church.

The "Sunday School celebration" was an annual event that helped to keep many schools going through months of discouragement and disappointment. In many communities of the last century, Sunday School associations owned "tabernacles." These were huge wooden shelters, supported by stout logs and having no sides. Seats were of pine boards, and a sawdust covering on the ground served as a floor.

The tabernacle was the site of the annual celebration, usually held in the spring. From miles around came the Sunday

A pioneer Sunday School.

School pupils and their leaders, on foot or horseback, in crude ox carts or gleaming carriages drawn by matched pairs.

The weather was warm, and fans fluttered to stir the faint breeze under the shelter. The scent of cinnamon, Hoyt's cologne, and hair oil was in the air.

First there were reports from each Sunday School represented. No matter how remote his school or how few his pupils, each superintendent was given his moment to report successes or failures. After an inspirational message or two came the highlights of the day—dinner.

Tables arranged around the edge of the tabernacle were covered with food. There were chicken salad, chicken pie, baked chicken, roast chicken, fried chicken. Cold boiled ham was brought from home smokehouses. Roast beef, barbecued beef, dried beef, and fried beef were offered. Pickles, sauces, and salads served to whet the appetite. And to top it all off, there were cakes and pies of all shapes, flavors, and designs—all home baked.

Men and boys were put to the test at these dinners. As they approached the tables, the women and girls urged upon them their own specialties. Woe to the swain who turned down a heaping portion of anything his girlfriend proffered!

The afternoon was given over to a singing contest for the association's coveted blue and silver banner. This banner had flown all day over the Sunday School that had won it in competition the year before.

Each school selected its song and a leader. Every member of a chorus was required to be a member in good standing of the Sunday School. After the judging, the winners were congratulated. Then all joined in a chorus of "God be with you till we meet again," and the celebration was over until the following spring.

TEMPERANCE Speaker Warned Of Wild, Tormented Beasts

Southern Baptists may be as nearly united in their public stand against the sale and use of alcoholic beverages as they are on any social issue. However, this stand has undergone much change over the years. It has ranged from open acceptance and use of alcohol to bitter denunciation.

The changing attitude toward alcohol is seen in this impassioned temperance speech before the Florida Baptist Convention early in this century.

> *"Time was when a man could drink whiskey to excess and defy the laws of God and man by living out his alloted span of life, but not today. For the whiskies and brandies and wines and beers of today are not those that our forefathers once kept in their decanters and gave to their guests and drank themselves. By no means, no. Those beverages were made from wholesome grain and apples and pears and peaches. But the intoxicating drinks of today are blends and decoctions, forged with the liquid fires of torment, and into them go the deadly night shade and aqua fortis and capudine and capesam and cayenne pepper, and the poisonous fusil oil. Into the lighter drinks of wine and beer there go the fumes of sulphuric and carbolic acid. The consequence is that men today do not know the comparatively harmless drink of ancient times, but when they become intoxicated on these fiery beverages they turn loose whole menageries of wild and tormented beasts into their maddened brains."*

BAPTISM Was Sometimes Hazardous

Baptists of an earlier day performed their baptisms in a stream or river, after the manner of Jesus' baptism by John the Baptist in the River Jordan.

While the practice was Scriptural and picturesque, it sometimes presented hazards. One Baptist preacher led a woman convert into a river for baptism. As they came up out of the water, the preacher saw a poisonous snake coiled on the robe the woman had left on the river bank. The preacher quickly seized the snake and hurled it to the other side of the river.

One of those who witnessed the baptism was amazed by the preacher's quickness of mind and hand. "Why, the apostle Paul could not have done more!" he exclaimed.

Actually, the preacher was either more fortunate or more agile than the apostle. Paul was bitten by a snake, but escaped unharmed (Acts 28).

LITTLE Money, Much Labor Built Churches of Earlier Day

It did not take a lot of money to build a church 100 years ago; it took only a lot of labor. And willing hands were one thing churches of that day had in abundance.

The church was made of pine logs, of course, cut from the forest and peeled of their bark. These were notched by ax and set in place by hand.

The roof was of shingles split from pine blocks and drawn, one at a time, by hand with a drawing knife. Benches were of logs, split and hewn, and fitted with legs driven into augur holes. Even the pulpit, framed of small hewn logs, was built of boards split with a froe or cleaving tool.

The door of the church opened onto an aisle which divided the rows of benches into two sections. In one section sat the men and boys; in the other section were the women and girls. In every open space a quilt was spread to make a pallet for a sleeping child.

Evening services were held at "candlelight." From cross joists in the unceiled building, kerosene lamps were swung. Their dim light fell on the congregation and filtered through

An early church in Missouri.

the cracks between the logs to the horses, mules, and oxen tethered outside with the wagons, buggies, and carts.

Baptisms were held in the afternoon, usually at a stream near the church. A favorite spot was where a road crossed a stream. The wheels of the wagons and the hooves of the animals made the river bottom there smooth and firm. A dressing room of poles and sheets or blankets was sometimes erected at the river bank so that women candidates could change clothes. The congregation gathered at the river bank to sing hymns and congratulate and encourage the new convert.

"There is a fountain filled with blood
Drawn from Immanuel's veins;
And sinners plunged beneath that flood
Lose all their guilty stains."

Although the sexes were carefully separated during the worship service, this did not interfere with courtship at church. Many fond glances were exchanged across the aisle during the service. The "meetinghouse" was a favorite gathering place for couples. After a daylight service a young swain would approach his favorite and ask for the privilege of "walking her home." Then the two of them would stroll down the three-rut road—two ruts made by wagon and buggy wheels and the third by the hoofs of the animals—to her home, perhaps five miles away.

Bibliography

A Narrative of the Life of David Crockett of the State of Tennessee, written by himself. Cincinnati: U. P. James, 1834.

Armitage, Thomas, *A History of the Baptists.* New York: Bryan Taylor and Co., 1886.

Armstrong, O. K., and Marjorie M., *The Indomitable Baptists.* Garden City, N. Y.: Doubleday, 1967.

Bacock, Rufus, *Memoir of John Mason Peck.* Philadelphia: American Baptist Publication Society, 1864.

Backus, Isaac, *The Church History of New England.* E. Lincoln, 1804.

Baker, Robert A., *A Baptist Source Book.* Nashville: Broadman Press, 1966.

———, *The Baptist March in History.* Nashville: Broadman Press, 1953.

———, *The Southern Baptist Convention and Its People.* Nashville: Broadman Press, 1974.

———, *The Story of the Sunday School Board.* Nashville: Convention Press, 1966.

Barnes, Lemuel Call; Barnes, Mary Clark; and Stephenson, Edward M., *Pioneers of Light.* Philadelphia: The American Baptist Publication Society, 1924.

Barnes, W. W., *The Southern Baptist Convention 1845-1953.* Nashville: Broadman Press, 1954.

Benedict, David, *50 Years Among the Baptists.* New York: Sheldon and Co., 1860.

Beverly, O. B., *A Brief History of the Woodville Baptist Church.*

Burkitt, Lemuel, and Read, Jesse, *A Concise History of Kehukee Baptist Association.* Philadelphia: Lippincott, 1850.

Carroll, J. M., *A History of Texas Baptists.* Dallas, Texas: Baptist Standard Publishing Co., 1923.

Cathcart, William, *The Baptist Encyclopedia.* Philadelphia: Louis H. Everts, 1881.

Carver, William O., *Out of His Treasure.* Nashville: Broadman Press, 1956.

Christian, John T., *A History of the Baptists.* Nashville: Sunday School Board of the Southern Baptist Convention, 1922.

Cox, Norman W., *Dreams, Dungeons, Diadems!* Nashville: Historical Commission of the Southern Baptist Convention, 1954.

Cox, Norman W., Editor, *Encyclopedia of Southern Baptists.* Nashville: Broadman Press, 1958.

Dick, Everett, *The Dixie Frontier.* New York: Alford A. Knopf, Inc., 1948.

Duncan, R. S., *A History of the Baptists in Missouri.* St. Louis: Scammell and Co., 1882.

Elliott, L. R., *Centennial Story of Texas Baptists.* Dallas, Texas: Baptist General Convention of Texas, 1936.

Filson, John, *The Discovery, Settlement and Present State of Kentucky.* New York: Corinth Books, Inc., 1962.

Fuller, B. F., *History of Texas Baptists.* Louisville, Ky.: Baptist Book

Concern, 1900.

Gambrell, J. B., *Ten Years in Texas*. Dallas, Tex.: The Baptist Standard, 1910.

Griffin, Charles M., *The Story of South Carolina Baptists, 1683-1933*. Walterboro, S. C.: Press of Connie Maxwell Orphanage, 1934.

Grime, J. H., *History of Middle Tennessee Baptists*. Nashville: Baptist and Reflector, 1902.

Harwell, Jack U., *An Old Friend with New Credentials*. Atlanta: The Christian Index, 1972.

Hatcher, William E., *Along the Trail of the Friendly Years*. New York: Fleming H. Revell Co., 1910.

Hays, Brooks, and Steely, John E., *The Baptist Way of Life*. Englewood Cliffs, N. J.: Prentice-Hall, Inc., 1963.

Heck, Fannie E. S., *In Royal Service*. Richmond, Va.: Foreign Mission Board, Southern Baptist Convention, 1928.

Herring, J. L., *Saturday Night Sketches*. Boston: The Gorham Press, 1918.

Herring, Reuben, *Seventeenth Century Baptist Press*. Nashville: Southern Baptist Historical Commission, 1955.

———, *Eighteenth Century Baptist Press*. Nashville: Southern Baptist Historical Commission, 1957.

———, *Nineteenth Century Baptist Press*. Nashville: Southern Baptist Historical Commission, 1959.

Holcombe, Hosea, *A History of the Rise and Progress of the Baptists in Alabama*. Philadelphia: King and Baird, 1840.

James, Charles F., *Documentary History of the Struggle for Religious Liberty in Virginia*. Lynchburg, Va.: J. P. Bell Co., 1900.

Joiner, Edward E., *A History of Florida Baptists*. Jacksonville, Fla.: Convention Press, Inc., 1972.

Knowles, James D., *Memoir of Roger Williams*. Boston: Lincoln, Edmands and Co., 1834.

Leavell, Z. T., and Baily, T. J., *A Complete History of Mississippi Baptists*. Jackson, Miss.: Mississippi Baptist Publishing Co., 1904.

Lester, James A., *A History of the Georgia Baptist Convention 1822-1972*. The Baptist Convention of the State of Georgia, 1972.

Little, Lewis P., *Imprisoned Preachers and Religious Liberty in Virginia*. Lynchburg, Va.: J. P. Bell Co., Inc., 1938.

Mallary, C. D., *Memoirs of Elder Jesse Mercer*. New York: J. Gray, 1844.

Masters, Frank M., *A History of Baptists in Kentucky*. Kentucky Baptist Historical Society, 1953.

May, Lynn E., *The First Baptist Church of Nashville, Tennessee, 1820-1970*. Nashville, 1970.

Mead, Frank S., *The Baptists*. Nashville: Broadman Press, 1954.

Morrell, Z. N., *Flowers and Fruits in the Wilderness*. St. Louis: Commercial Printing Co., 1872.

Mosteller, James D., *A History of the Kiokee Baptist Church in Georgia*. Ann Arbor, Mich.: Edwards Bros., Inc., 1952.

Newman, A. H., *A History of the Baptist Churches in the United States*. New York: The Christian Literature Co., 1894.

Paschal, C. W., *History of the North Carolina Baptists*. Raleigh, N. C.: North Carolina Baptist State Convention, 1930.

Patterson, W. Morgan, *Successionism: a Critical View*. Valley Forge: Judson Press, 1969.

Paxton, W. E., *A History of the Baptists of Louisiana*. St. Louis: C. R. Barnes Publishing Co., 1888.

Pendleton, J. M., *Reminiscences of a Long Life*. Louisville, Ky.: Press Baptist Book Concern, 1891.

Pitts, Charles F., *Chaplains in Gray*. Nashville: Broadman Press, 1957.

Pollard, E. G., and Stevens, D. G., *Luther Rice, Pioneer in Missions and Education*. Philadelphia: Judson Press, 1928.

Posey, Walter B., *The Baptist Church in the Lower Mississippi Valley 1776-1845*. Lexington, Ky.: University of Kentucky Press, 1957.

Purefoy, George W., *A History of the Sandy Creek Baptist Association*.

New York: Sheldon & Co., 1859.

Riley, B. F., *A History of the Baptists in the Southern States East of the Mississippi*. Philadelphia: American Baptist Publication Society, 1898.

———, *A Memorial History of the Baptists of Alabama*. Philadelphia: Judson Press, 1923.

———, *History of the Baptists of Texas*. Dallas, Tex.: 1907.

Rogers, J. S., *History of Arkansas Baptists*. Little Rock, Ark.: Arkansas Baptist State Convention, 1948.

Ross, James, *Life and Times of Elder Reuben Ross*. Philadelphia: Grant, Faires and Rodgers, 1882.

Ryland, Garnett, *The Baptists of Virginia, 1697-1926*. Richmond, Va.: Baptist Board of Missions and Education, 1955.

Semple, Robert B., *A History of the Rise and Progress of the Baptists in Virginia*. Richmond, Va.: Pitt and Dickinson, 1894.

Shurden, Walter B., *Not a Silent People: Controversies That Shaped Southern Baptists*. Nashville: Broadman Press, 1972.

St. Amant, C. P., *A Short History of Louisiana Baptists*. Nashville: Broadman Press, 1948.

Sweet, William W., *Religion in the Development of American Culture 1765-1840*. New York: Charles Scribner's Sons, 1952.

———, *Religion on the American Frontier, the Baptists, 1783-1830*. New York: Henry Holt, Inc., 1933.

———, *Religion on the American Frontier, the Presbyterians, 1783-1840*. New York: Harper and Bros., 1936.

Taylor, James B., *Memoir of Rev. Luther Rice*. Nashville: Broadman Press, 1841; rev., 1937.

Taylor, John, *History of Ten Baptist Churches*. Frankfort, Ky.: J. H. Holeman, 1823.

Taylor, O. W., *Early Tennessee Baptists, 1769-1832*. Nashville: Tennessee Baptist Convention, 1957.

The First Baptist Church, Richmond, Virginia, 1780-1955. Richmond, Va.: Whittet and Shepperson, 1955.

Torbet, R. G., *A History of the Baptists*. Philadelphia: The Judson Press, 1952.

Vedder, Henry C., *A Short History of the Baptists*. Philadelphia: The American Baptist Publication Society, 1907.

Wallis, Charles L., *Autobiography of Peter Cartwright*. Nashville: Abingdon Press, 1956.

Weaver, R. W., *The Place of Luther Rice in American Baptist Life*. Washington, D.C.: The Luther Rice Centennial Commission, 1936.

Williams, Charles B., *A History of the Baptists in North Carolina*. Raleigh, N. C.: Presses of Edwards & Broughton, 1901.

Woolley, Davis C., *Baptist Advance*. Nashville: Broadman Press, 1964.

The author is indebted to the personnel of the Southern Baptist Historical Commission and the Dargan-Carver Library of the Sunday School Board for making available their extensive facilities and resources, including microfilm, minutes, journals, correspondence, photographs, drawings, and other memorabilia.

INDEX TO TOPICS

The Lash of Persecution

The Struggle for Religious Freedom

The Call of the Frontier

The Fight Between Brothers

The Pangs of Growth